HOW TO GO
FROM RAGS TO RICHES <u>FAST</u> WITH SOUND REAL ESTATE INVESTMENTS

HOW TO GO
FROM RAGS TO
RICHES <u>FAST</u> WITH SOUND
REAL ESTATE INVESTMENTS

J. Brad Lampley

PRENTICE-HALL, INC.

Englewood Cliffs, N. J.

Prentice-Hall International, Inc., *London*
Prentice-Hall of Australia, Pty. Ltd., *Sydney*
Prentice-Hall of Canada, Ltd., *Toronto*
Prentice-Hall of India Private Ltd., *New Delhi*
Prentice-Hall of Japan., Inc., *Tokyo*

© 1974 by

J. Brad Lampley

All rights reserved. No part of this book may be reproduced in any form or by any means, without permission in writing from the publisher.

Library of Congress Cataloging in Publication Data

Lampley, J. Brad,
   How to go from rags to riches fast with sound real estate investments.

   1. Real estate investment. 2. Real estate investment--United States. I. Title.
HD1375.L35   332.6'324'0973   73-19780
ISBN 0-13-409771-8

Printed in the United States of America

Introduction

My decision to write this book was based on a series of events which took place after my retirement from active participation as an investor and as a Realtor. In spite of the fact that I knew very well that the real estate market was on the threshhold of a tremendous boom, and quite possibly one of the most formidable booms to come along in many years, at the age of 36 I sold my real estate practice and enlisted my successors to handle the professional management of my real estate holdings. My intentions were to spend a great deal of time traveling and leading the good life, with an eye to writing fiction, which has long been my desire.

I soon discovered, however, that when I was at home I received a constant flood of calls from friends, former clients, and other people referred to me for advice on the different aspects of real estate investment. My first impulse was to start an investment consultation service, which could have been of invaluable service to many investors; but since I did not wish to get involved with another business, my next choice was to write a book covering the essential information necessary for sound real estate investment with a high degree of success. In that way, I could give everyone who cared to read the book the advantage of my wide real estate experience.

The intent of this book is to give you the tools with which to start at the bottom—with virtually no money if that be the case—and to go all the way to the top of the financial ladder through investments in real estate. In other words, to provide the tools with which you can reach your financial goal, whether it be to accumulate a cool million dollars; a comfortable early retirement; extensive first class travel (perhaps on your own yacht); or simply to "do your own thing" with the knowledge that your financial worries are over.

There is no end to what could be written on the subject of real estate investments. In order to cover every eventuality, and all the detailed knowledge which could be helpful, it would require writing several volumes consisting of thousands of pages. But to do that would be to burden you with more details than you could possibly follow with any reasonable degree of effectiveness. So in order to strive for maximum effectiveness with a minimum of confusion, I have condensed the contents to cover what I consider to be the most important points, getting down to the nitty-gritty on how to make the plan work for you.

For the sake of simplicity and to make the instructions easy to follow, I have attempted to list the contents in the order in which you will need them, so that you may advance to succeeding stages at your own pace. Your ability to progress successfully through the various stages will depend on many things, not the least of which is how hard you are willing to work at it. The amount of work necessary will depend a great deal on the amount of cash you have on hand to begin with, but it will depend to a larger extent on how well you are equipped with the basic information necessary for successful investment. A little knowledge is good, but a lot of knowledge is essential for consistent success in the real estate investment field. So prepare yourself well. It's worth the effort. It will save you a lot of grief, as well as clear your road to success.

So, armed with the knowledge which has taken me almost ten years to acquire (most of which I experienced personally, with the balance learned through observing the success and failures of others), it should be a relatively easy process for you to reach your goal, whatever it may be.

J. Brad Lampley

CONTENTS

Introduction 5

1. Can Anyone Get Rich Quick in Real Estate? 15
    Does Success Require Speculation? 16
    How Much Depends on Luck? 17
    When Is the Right Time to Buy? 17
    Am I Either Too Young or Too Old? 18

2. Can I Succeed in My Spare Time? 20
    Do I Need a Real Estate License? 21
    A License Can Be a Disadvantage 21

3. How to Select a Good Location for Investments 25
    The Best Prospects 25
    Concentrate on One Area 26
        Is the area going up hill or down?—What percentage of the properties have absentee owners?—Are there many real estate brokers in the area?
    There Are Always Opportunities 32

4. Selecting an Agent 34
    Listing Your Property with an Agent 37
    Should I Bypass the Broker? 39

5. How to Determine the Best Price 43
    Appraising the Single-Family Dwelling 47
        In a relatively new area with primarily new houses:—In an area with a preponderance of old houses:—
    Appraising Income Property 51
        Analyzing the income as a prospective buyer:— Analyzing the income as a seller:—

6. Sources of Good Buys 62

    Avoid Commercial Property   63

    Forget "I Could Live in It If Things Get Tough."   64

    Avoid Real Estate Syndications   65

    Avoid Resort Properties as Investments   65

    So, How and Where Do I Find the Good Buys?   66

7. Profit Advantages of Condominiums 75

    Dangers of Over-Expansion   76

    The Cluster Concept   77

        The fourplex condominium—Financing the condominium project

    No Quick Profit in a New Condominium   79

    Where Are the Good Buys?   79

        Used units in older condominiums—Converting apartment buildings

    Appealing Aspects—Who Buys Condominiums?   81

        Attract the senior citizens—Good rentals make good condominiums—The setting must catch the eye

    Conversion Pointers   84

    Your First Investment—Make It a Small One   88

8. Preparing Your Property for Sale 90

    Appearances Count   90

    Avoid Unnecessary Costs   91

    Limit Your Remodeling   91

9. Getting Involved with a Partner 93

    A Silent Partner Is Best   93

    Joint Ownership   94

CONTENTS 11

10. Property Management **98**
    Don't Ignore Tenant Complaints   98
    Find the Right Manager   99

11. The Importance of Income Tax Guidance **109**
    Impractical Selling   109
    Sale of Personal Residence   111
    Learn about Capital Gains   112
    Plan Your Taxes   113

12. Financing **115**
    Don't Be Afraid of Junior Mortgages   116
    Don't Be Afraid to Borrow Money   117
    Prime Sources of Financing   118
    What about Balloon Payments?   120

13. Remodeling **122**
    Making the Right Improvements   123
    Decorating   126

14. How to Negotiate **129**
    To Buy   129
> *Price and terms to offer—Don't act anxious—Keep your deposit small—Regarding private financing—Watch out for possible leases— Know what is included in the price —Title insurance is a must—Take into consideration the seller's reason for selling—*

    To Sell   139
> *Set your own price—Make the property available—Watch for phony offers—Avoiding the contingency pitfalls—Get the buyer while he's hot—Don't be an interest hog—Don't always insist on an all-cash sale*

15. Getting Started with Little or No Cash **149**

Getting Started with Little or No Cash (*Continued*)

    The Importance of Good Credit   150

    Sources of Cash or Its Equivalent   152

    Acquiring Property under a Lease-Option   154

    The Cost of Securing an Option to Purchase   156

    The Agreement of Sale   159

    Other Important Points to Consider   161

16. Minimum Cash Investment **166**

    How to Generate Cash for the Down Payment   167

    How Much Should I Allow for Closing Costs?   171

    What Type of Property Should I Start With?   176

    Doubling Your Money   178

17. Ways to Protect Your Cash Investments **180**

    Tax Advantages of Real Estate Ownership   181

    The Tax Free Exchange   181

    Will the Improvements Pay for Themselves?   184

    The Importance of Leverage   185

    Pyramiding   185

    Looking for Long-Term Investments   190

    General Words of Caution   191

18. Preparing for Retirement **193**

    Sell on the Installment Plan   194

    Hire a Management Firm   194

Real Estate Terms **196**

Index **207**

HOW TO GO FROM RAGS TO RICHES FAST WITH SOUND REAL ESTATE INVESTMENTS

1

Can Anyone Get Rich Quick in Real Estate?

Yes, you too can reach your goal of financial independence by investing in real estate. That is, providing your desire to attain that goal is real and that you are willing to go about your task in a systematic manner. If you tend to be conservative in your approach and you follow the rules of the game, there is little reason to be concerned about failure or serious setbacks. You may rise a little more slowly than the hasty individual, but your success will be more assured.

If, on the other hand, you are impatient to get to the top and are willing to take large risks, then you may achieve your goal far ahead of my program by applying the principles of pyramiding to their full potential. But if you choose this path, which I do not advocate for most investors, be prepared to lose and do not invest more than you are willing to lose. For while risky investments can reap large and immediate rewards, by the same token they can cause the loss of an entire investment. So, along this line, beware and good luck.

DOES SUCCESS REQUIRE SPECULATION?

Most people classify real estate investments that are designed for substantial or quick profits in the category of speculation. However, I would not use that term for what I am proposing. I would just call it investing, because speculation implies a considerable degree of risk. I have never made an investment in real estate that I thought carried a high degree of risk. For the most part, I did not feel that there was any risk at all. Even under the worst of conditions, such as a depression, I felt I would have been able to hold on to most or all of my investments. In 1966, the bottom practically fell out of the real estate financial market, creating a severe shortage of funds and resultant hardship—even disaster—for many investors who had been flying high for many years. But most of the people who fell by the wayside were over-extended, as is usually the case with unwary speculators. The ensuing difficult times, which had severe effects on the financing and marketability of many of the most desirable investment properties, lasted for several years and only achieved a substantial recovery in 1971. During that difficult real estate market, I did not at any time have difficulty either in maintaining adequate funds or in the successful operation of my real estate holdings. In fact, it was quite the opposite.

I was just beginning to get a good foothold in the market, in 1966, when the tight money situation came about—I was about ready to start "wheeling and dealing." But because of the difficulties brought about by the tight money market, I decided to reevaluate the situation and embark on a more conservative course, which I believe turned out to be the best course.

HOW MUCH DEPENDS ON LUCK?

For the most part I have not found luck playing an important part in successful investment in real estate. Obviously, there are times when either good or bad luck can affect the opportunities available to you, or the outcome of your investments. But luck alone is not enough, since you must have your mind attuned in order to recognize good luck. If you are not alert, good luck will pass you by. I have had many people tell me, "you sure are lucky." But the fact is, I was fortunate enough to recognize good opportunities when I saw them, whereas many of my colleagues and clients were letting that same "luck" pass them by.

WHEN IS THE RIGHT TIME TO BUY?

Any time is the right time to buy. Don't sit around waiting to start investing because you are afraid there might be a depression, or a recession, or some such problem. The chances are that there will not be a depression. There are a lot of checks and balances now in effect which serve to give virtual assurance against another serious depression. At any rate, if you start investing now and are successful in building substantial investment equity, even with the advent of a depression you would most surely salvage a lot more than you would have accumulated with your savings sitting in a bank collecting a comparatively low rate of interest. So how can you lose?

As for the recurring recessions, don't worry about them. If you try to wait for the most opportune time to invest, the best time will no doubt be gone before you recognize it. In any event, by waiting you will have lost a lot of valuable time in which you could have substantially increased your assets. Moreover, the longer you wait, the higher price you will pay when you do buy.

As an example, during my years as a Realtor, I encountered many unhappy prospective investors who were waiting for the right time or the right price. Often, they were afraid that the economy was headed in the wrong direction. But more often, they thought that the price was too high. Many times I have heard it said, "I saw this building several years ago (sometimes as much as ten years before) when it was only such-and-such a price (often less than one-half the asking price at the time of my showing)." They would further relate, "I wish I had bought it then, but I thought the price was too high."

In talking further with these people, I would usually discover that they had been looking for an investment for many years without having made a single purchase. In my opinion, if anyone has been looking for a real estate investment for over six months without success, then it is time to sit down and take a close look at the situation to see where the problem lies. If, after an extended search, you have not found a property that you feel would serve your purpose, then you are off base somewhere.

The days of opportunity are never over. They are sometimes changed by temporary market conditions and you need only to recognize them.

AM I EITHER TOO YOUNG OR TOO OLD?

You are never too young or too old.

If you are too young for your signature to be accepted in order to form a binding agreement, then you can still invest if someone (preferably a member of your family) is willing to stand behind you. That can get complicated, however, and is not advisable unless you are prepared to take more than the usual precaution to make sure that you are well-informed and prepared to compete with the more mature and experienced investors in the market.

You are not too old if you are in good health and sound of mind. It does not take very long to accumulate a sizable nest egg, but if you are approaching what is referred to as old age then, obviously, you should proceed with more caution than you would if you were younger. If you make a mistake, you will have less time to make up for it later.

Also, do not invest your entire life savings. A reasonable approach would be to invest an amount which you can afford to get along without, just in case, and pyramid that investment until you reach your ultimate goal. That course of action is also advisable to most beginning investors, of any age, as I will explain later in more detail.

2

Can I Succeed in My Spare Time?

Should I keep my job and handle my investments on a part time basis, or should I quit my job and apply all my time to my real estate investments? The answer depends, of course, a great deal on your financial position. But generally, in the beginning you should keep your job. A job will be a valuable asset in more ways than one. First, it will help you to qualify for the necessary loans. Also, a steady income will help to cover remodeling costs, as well as providing the day-to-day living expenses, thereby making it possible for you to reinvest most, or all, of your gains. In fact, you should restrain yourself from increasing your standard of living too much as you progress, until you have reached a comfortable level where you have adequate investment funds to carry forward.

The spare time available to the average person, after fulfilling the obligations of a regular job, is quite adequate to handle a considerable volume of real estate investments. For example, even though I was not tied down to a job requiring regulated hours, throughout my entire real estate investment career the larger portion of my time was actually spent in the capacity of a real estate broker assisting my clients, rather than actually handling my own business interests. My investment activities were squeezed in between the wants and needs of my clients. However, at some point after you have established yourself in the business, you may wish to quit your regular job in order to devote more time to your investments.

DO I NEED A REAL ESTATE LICENSE?

It is not necessary to have a real estate license or to be employed in any phase of the real estate profession in order to be a highly successful investor in real estate. In fact, having a license could interfere with your personal investments. The primary advantage of having a license, particularly for the beginner with limited investment funds, is that you can apply the commission toward your down payment, thus reducing the amount of cash required for the investment. However, the full commission can often be obtained to apply as part of the down payment, even for the investor who does not have a license—as I'll explain in more detail later. Another advantage of having a license is that sometimes you have early access to potential investments as they become available and before they are snapped up by someone else.

A LICENSE CAN BE A DISADVANTAGE

The disadvantages of having a license, while making a career of real estate investing, are numerous. In most, and possibly all, areas of the United States, if you are licensed to sell real estate, then you are required by law to divulge to the prospective seller or purchaser that you are licensed and to reveal the exact nature of your interest in any particular transaction.

This requirement often extends to divulging at what price you plan to sell the property you are attempting to purchase. You can see the potential effect of this knowledge when a substantial price difference is involved. Also, many sellers feel that their price is too low if a real estate agent is purchasing the property. This is very often the case, even when the price is, in fact, quite as high as the market will bear.

As a licensee, you will sometimes find yourself in the position of representing the seller or purchaser (hereafter often referred to as the principal) at the same time you want to represent yourself. Your fiduciary responsibility to the principal can make it difficult, or impossible, for you to handle the transaction to your best advantage.

One of the most common problems for agents who want to invest for themselves is that they get so involved in trying to meet the needs of their clients that there is little or no time left for their own interests, particularly for the individual who is inclined to be conscientious in his work. In fact, as an agent, I always offered what I considered to be the best investment to every client who I thought might be interested, regardless of the fact that it might seem to be the best investment I was likely to come across for some time, and that I might like to purchase it for my own account. However, after presenting the "good deal' to everyone else, it was usually still available, since most investors overlook most good investments.

Without a license, if you have a good agent working for your interests, you will still have access to adequate "good buys." But don't rely too heavily on an agent for good investment opportunities. You should watch the newspaper ads and keep your eyes peeled for new "for sale" signs in the area that you have chosen for your investments.

After what I have said on the subject, if you are still interested in becoming licensed to sell real estate, then call or write the nearest state government office, care of the Real Estate Commissioner, for information and instructions on how to go about getting your license. Or consult the yellow pages of your local telephone directory under the heading Real Estate Schools. If none is listed, then check with the nearest major city. The school you should attend for the purpose of getting your real estate license is not usually a college or university, but a school that teaches only for the purpose of passing the necessary state examinations.

The time it will take to get your license will vary from state to state because of the varying requirements of state examinations. But on the average, the longest it should take to complete the necessary course and pass the examination is approximately three months. However, classes are usually designed so that you may progress at your own pace and some students complete the studies in much less than average time, while many others take considerably longer. The courses are usually offered in either day or night classes. The cost of the course varies a great deal, but is usually less than $250. Some prospective employers (real estate offices) will pay the school fee in order to get you to work for them, particularly if they think you will make a good sales person. It could be worth checking into.

Selecting an employing broker is a hit-and-miss proposition. Ideally, you should locate with a progressive office where new ideas are welcome and encouraged. If, after a fair trial at one office, you feel that you are not going to learn much from your experience there, or that the office will not be cooperative in lending you its share of commissions to assist in your investments, then do not hesitate to change offices. But, don't blame your problems or lack of success on the office. If you are doing your job right, and with the right attitude, you should have a reasonable degree of success regardless of what office you work with—particularly as regards your own investments.

Don't be shy or hesitant to apply at any office that you feel might be right for you. Most offices are always anxious to take on more salespeople—though some do not accept inexperienced or part-time associates.

3

How to Select a Good Location for Investments

The best service you can render yourself, right from the beginning, is to make sure that you are thoroughly familiar with all aspects of a location before you invest in it. This need not be a tedious chore. It is a matter of getting out and looking at as much real estate as possible and evaluating what you have seen so that you will be aware of what makes an investment either good or bad, or just fair. The key is to compare, compare, and compare. Don't worry if it happens to boggle your mind at first. Just stick with it and it will start to fit together a lot sooner than you think.

THE BEST PROSPECTS

The best area in which to locate properties with good potential for upgrading—which is the meat of what this book is all about—is a somewhat older area with many different styles and types of structures. Such areas usually contain many neglected buildings, or buildings in need of remodeling or decorating. The older areas also offer more opportunity for the investor to use his skill at detecting properties which are priced below market value; because the older and more varied the area, the more difficult it is to determine a price simply by comparison with other properties. So, if you know what you are doing, you will be able to recognize the best prospects, while your competitors are passing them by.

Another advantage is that the amenities vary more in old houses than in relatively new ones. In addition, your decorating ability will reap higher rewards in old houses because the appraisal rule of a certain number of dollars per square feet of floor space is not so closely adhered to in older buildings, thus leaving leeway for the price to be determined more by the individual appeal of the building concerned. Also, as a whole, old buildings have more potential for changes that could substantially increase their value.

It is relatively difficult to find a grossly underpriced property in a fairly new area. For one thing, the seller probably has not owned the property very long; thus you must contend with the price he paid for it. Further, it usually takes quite a number of years for property to become sufficiently out-dated or deteriorated to provide a substantial rehabilitation opportunity. There may be reasonable or good buys in the newer areas, but as a rule they do not offer the opportunity for the large capital gains that are available in older neighborhoods.

CONCENTRATE ON ONE AREA

One of the most important things to remember is that you cannot, in a short time, become sufficiently familiar with every area in a large city to be able to make good judgments about investments. So, decide on an area of the city that you think would be good for investments and concentrate on it until you have a thorough knowledge of what to expect in the way of prices in that area—keeping in mind the other important pointers mentioned throughout this book. Later on, after you have made several successful investments, you may want to consider expanding your knowledge to another area so as not to have all your investments in one place.

The qualities to look for in evaluating an area can best be found by asking yourself:

1. Is the area going up hill or down?

This concern is especially important when you are looking for an investment to hold for several years. It is also important in trying to make a quick sale, if the area is going downhill and that fact, or belief, is known to the real estate agents who service the area or by a good percentage of prospective purchasers. Most buyers avoid declining areas like the plague, which makes for lower prices. If you are unable to determine which direction the area is headed on your own, then you could start by contacting some agents in the vicinity and looking at as many properties as possible. Keep your eyes open and listen attentively. Ask questions, keeping in mind that many agents are not well-informed or have bad judgment, and also many more of them will not necessarily give you a straight answer to your questions. This is an important point to remember during all your contacts with agents. That is not to say that real estate agents are dishonest. There are dishonest people in the business the same as in any other business, and not necessarily more or less of them But when there is substantial money at stake, an agent's reasoning may be warped. As a result, even the most honest agent can easily make incorrect or misleading statements.

I am not suggesting that you go around on the defensive, but that you should be alert and evaluate everything you hear. This caution should be extended perhaps even more toward the principals involved in real estate transactions. During my extensive contacts in the business, I have discovered that many principals frequently make incorrect, misleading, or grossly exaggerated statements regarding their properties.

2. What percentage of the properties have absentee owners?

You can easily determine the percentage of absentee owners by checking with the Tax Accessor's Office. It should have available to the public a complete list of all property owners' names and mailing addresses. If an owner's mailing address is other than the property address, then that owner is usually an absentee owner—though owners sometimes list their office addresses for mailing purposes. This concern applies primarily to areas containing an abundance of single-family or small multiple-family dwellings, since most such buildings are traditionally occupied by the owners. You cannot necessarily apply the same yardstick to apartment buildings, since owners of apartment buildings usually do not live in them.

The reason for the importance of knowing whether or not the area has a large percentage of absentee owners is that there is a tendency for absentee owners to be less attentive to needed maintenance, especially exterior painting and repairs, with the result that the properties deteriorate more than they would if they were owner-occupied. This situation will eventually lead to a run-down appearance for the neighborhood as a whole.

There are many areas of neglect not directly related to the owner's attitude. It is a well-known fact that most tenants do not take as good care of the property they rent as they would if they owned it. Tenants seldom take proper care of the yards, if the task is left to them. Most tenants do not make an effort to keep the sidewalks free of debris, and this, often, also applies to the yards.

I have also discovered through experience that most tenants cause more general wear and tear on property than would an owner. So it all adds up, and in the end the whole area can suffer from the lack of a good general appearance. This, coupled with many absentee owners' reluctance to perform needed maintenance and repairs, will eventually cause an appearance of blight in the area.

3. Are there many real estate brokers in the area?

The most popular areas, where there is a large demand and a considerable turnover in sales, are where you will also find the largest concentration of brokers. It's a simple fact of life that the brokers have to earn a living, so if they are concentrated in any given area, then that is enough assurance that property in that area is selling at a fairly rapid pace. It also indicates that once you have made an investment in that area and are ready to sell it, there will be a demand for your product.

There will also be a lot of brokers to help sell your property, which will not only make it easier to sell, but you will most likely receive a good price in fairly short order. Competition among brokers usually results in elevated real estate prices. Of course, most brokers work in more than one area, but they will usually concentrate more heavily in the area where they are located. They usually locate in that area in the first place because they know there is a lot of activity and, once there, it is simply a matter of convenience to concentrate the larger part of their efforts on it.

So the easiest and probably the surest way to select a progressive area, where you can look forward to a quick turnover when necessary, is to look for an area with a large concentration of real estate brokers.

In winding up the discussion on how to select an area for your investments, I would like to make some final points that you should watch closely:

Stay away from government redevelopment areas. There are some seemingly attractive lures to invest in redevelopment areas, such as low-interest loans for rehabilitation and improvements, rapid depreciation writeoffs for low income rentals, and so forth. But in my opinion, the disadvantages far outweigh the advantages. Every time I considered getting involved with property where I would be forced to contend with a redevelopment agency, the amount of red tape involved invariably caused me to decide against the project.

There were other more viable reasons for my shying away from the redevelopment projects. It is impossible to predict the rate of progress one can expect, since government-sponsored projects are so vulnerable to problems with funding and other political maneuvering. In San Francisco, for example, one of the large redevelopment projects got under way in 1957 with massive demolition of old buildings. The entire project, which covered a large area of the city, was scheduled for completion in a matter of a few years. But to this date, that same project is no more than half-completed, if even that. The delays are totally unpredictable, what with every personal interest group in the area, and some outside it, haggling continuously with anyone who has anything to do with the project, all the way from City Hall on down through the ranks of building contractors and their employees.

Another serious problem is that the redevelopment agency's rehabilitation requirements are so extensive, requiring a lot of unnecessary work which does not enhance the value of the property, that the resultant costs often cause the total cost of the property to exceed its market value. And since your goal is to make a profit on your investment, and as quickly as possible, I strongly suggest that you avoid the redevelopment areas.

Another point is to be on guard for the area boundaries which would put your investment in or too near an undesirable location. It is often difficult to tell where a desirable area begins and ends. I have seen many areas where a person could make an investment with excellent prospects of selling it for a handsome profit, with no noticeable buyer resistance to the area; when just around the corner in the next block the same building would have been next to impossible to sell at even a substantially reduced price. There are many reasons for this type of situation. The following is a partial list of some of the things to look for:

A. Do most of the other buildings in the block present a good appearance, and are they of approximately equal quality or appearance as the building you are considering purchasing? If not, then your prospective investment may be an over-improvement for the area. This will be covered in more detail later

B. Does the block have an attractive or impressive appearance as a whole? This may not be necessary, depending on the quality and price of your prospective investment, but it should be considered.

C. How is the automobile traffic on the street? This is particularly important if you expect to sell your investment to a family with small children. If it is a through street with one way traffic, it is usually more traveled, and at higher speeds—even if it is a fairly small street—thus offering more cause for considering the possible objections that prospective buyers might raise

D. Perhaps most important—is the particular block you are considering near the fringe of an area which is going down in value, or is it near an already undesirable area? If so, the price should be adjusted accordingly, and even then you should be prepared for the fact that the property might be slow to sell. Sometimes a good area can expand into a bad area, and I have had a great deal of experience in such situations. But the predominant trend is that the bad areas are the ones which are expanding.

THERE ARE ALWAYS OPPORTUNITIES

There will always be ample opportunity to make profitable real estate investments. Regardless of the market conditions in general, the opportunities are always there, everywhere in all parts of the United States and the world. It is only the technique or approach that must be changed and tailored to fit the existing situation. My proposals do not include the need for good luck or any particular skill beyond using reasonably good judgment and plain common sense, in conjunction with basic know-how, which I propose to provide.

Ideally, in order to experience maximum appreciation on your investments it is best to be situated in an area with substantial population growth. Growth creates demand, which can be an important factor in pushing prices up. But population growth is by no means essential. In fact, the population of San Francisco, where I made practically all of my investments, has been on the decline for over a decade (from 740,000 in 1960 to 704,000 in 1970), while at the same time property values have kept pace with most other areas which have experienced substantial population growth.

A declining population does not erase the opportunity for good investment, but its potential impact may need to be taken into consideration. Many areas experience temporary population losses as a result of changing industrial demand on the labor force. This type of change will provide good investment opportunities for the alert investor who is looking ahead two or three years, when things will pick up again.

4

Selecting an Agent

One thing that will have a profound effect on how much assistance you will get from an agent is how well the agent likes you. It's human nature and it will work here too. So put your best foot forward when you encounter a broker. But don't let your vanity get the best of you—don't forget that a good broker will usually be doing the same thing. He may make you feel as if you are his long-lost brother. And it could be that he does genuinely like you, but don't let that lower your guard to the point where you will jump at his advice or be smooth-talked into a deal you're not sure you want.

Do not expect to stick with the first agent you run across when you start looking at real estate. It will probably take some time before you will be qualified to judge whether a broker has the qualifications necessary to do the best job.

You will find that many brokers do not have the faintest notion of what they are doing. They are simply stabbing in the dark, and as a result they usually come up with nothing of any real value. If a broker is not fully aware of the market, then he will waste a lot of your time. And if you let such a person lead you around, the chances are that you will

SELECTING AN AGENT

learn nothing worthwhile and will come across very few, if any, good investments.

It is usually advisable not to get too involved with brokers who have been in the real estate field for a long period of time, say 30 years or more, since they tend to get set in their ways and do not adjust with the changing market. It is also best to avoid a broker who has been in the real estate business for less than a year or so, since he is not likely to know enough to be of much help to you. You need someone with enough experience to weed out the properties which would obviously not suit your purposes.

In order for any broker, no matter how perceptive he may be, to find the right investment, it will be necessary for you to explain to him what you want, and most of all to be perfectly frank about it. If you do not tell the broker your honest opinion of a property he has shown you, how is he to learn any more about what you want? So tell him what you like, and just as frankly what you don't like, about the properties he has shown you.

On the other hand, if you do not know exactly what you want, then tell him so and explain as best you can. Then, if after several outings with a broker, he is still showing you properties that do not even remotely resemble what you want, it is time to consider getting another broker, or possibly analyzing your approach to see whether you have given him any help. Also consider the possibility that what you want may not be available. With your proper assistance, some brokers will catch on right away and can be very helpful, while others are so incompetent they will never be of any real help.

You should try to select a broker whose office is located in the general vicinity that you have chosen for your investments. As a seeker of good values, the very best broker for you is the one who personally obtains a lot of exclusive listings on properties. The broker who continuously canvasses prospective sellers for listings will be more likely to come up with some properties that have not been on the market for a long time. Among these listings will be some of the best opportunities, and if you are working directly with the listing broker, then you have a fair chance of getting the first crack at purchasing the property.

But the best advice would be to use the services of several brokers. Using only one broker will be too restrictive, just as using too many brokers will be counter-productive since it will be impossible to get across to all of them what you want, and you will be burdened with looking at too many properties which do not meet your needs.

In any case, a good broker will most surely be one who is hard at work; one who gets around enough to find the best opportunities and, more important, can recognize them when he sees them. Not many good investment opportunities just drop into your lap. Either you or your broker will have to go out and find them.

There is a lot that could be said about unscrupulous brokers, but it would be next to impossible to describe all the methods used by them in such a way as to be helpful to you. The name of the game is to beware. As a seller, don't be taken in by the broker who tells you that he has a buyer for your property. He may leave the impression that the property is as good as sold, when his immediate goal is just to get the listing signed. I learned about the use of this technique from clients who had been taken in by it.

The fact that a broker is misleading you along these lines does not, however, mean that he would not do a good job selling your property. It's just that you should realize that he probably does not have a buyer on hand. With this clear understanding, you will be able to make a more objective decision as to what kind of listing you should give out on the property, and to whom it should be given.

As a buyer, don't be talked into signing an offer unless you are ready, and don't fall for the old line that the property will be sold if you wait until later to make up your mind. You will sometimes need to take that chance, in order to take the necessary precautions against making a mistake.

In short, if you use your common sense, plus intuition, you should be able to sum up the situation with little difficulty. In fact, if you listen attentively, you will probably learn a lot from a shady broker—mostly in terms of what not to do or how not to be caught on the short end of a deal. If you are too unsure about certain aspects of a deal, just let it pass. When in doubt about its legal aspects, seek the advice of a real estate attorney. However, do not seek advice from an attorney regarding the correct price to be paid for a property.

LISTING YOUR PROPERTY WITH AN AGENT

When you are ready to sell your property, you will need all the help you can get from agents. If you have a strong feeling that a particular agent will market your property in such a way as to produce the best results to be reasonably expected, then it is all right to give an exclusive listing—even for a 90-day period, if that much time is required in order to get the property listed with the multiple listing service. Unless, of course, you are in a real hurry to sell the property.

If time is critical, it might be best to give only a 30-day listing, with the understanding that you will consider, but not guarantee, renewing the listing when it expires. In this way, the agent will be more likely to push the property, rather than let it sit around with the hope that "it just might sell." But even when you give a 90-day listing, a good way to give the agent a little push without offending him is to give him the impression that you may not be interested in selling the property if it is not sold promptly. Especially if the property is vacant, you can use the excuse that keeping it vacant for more than 30 to 40 days would cause a hardship and that it might be necessary to withdraw the listing in the event the property is not sold during that period.

If you are anxious for the property to sell, which may often be the case, it might be better to give out a 30-day open (or non-exclusive) listing. An open listing obligates you to pay a commission to the agent only if you sell the property to someone whose attention was brought to your property as a result of the agent's efforts (this obligation could vary depending on the wording in the open listing agreement). It can get a little tricky though, since you could unknowingly sell the property directly to an unscrupulous buyer who had been referred to your property by the agent, in which case you could be responsible to the agent for a commission you had not counted on. So, as always, read carefully the wording of your agreement so you will know what to watch for in order to protect yourself.

When selling a property yourself, have the buyer sign some kind of statement to the effect that he was not referred by a real estate agent from the office, or offices (specify the company by name) that have had a signed open listing on the property. An open listing can be given out to more than one broker, while at the same time you have the right to sell the property yourself.

When giving an exclusive listing, always make sure that you have a clear understanding with the listing agent, preferably in writing, that full cooperation is to be extended to all other brokers who may wish to participate. The broker has a fiduciary responsibility to the seller to make every reasonable effort to procure a buyer for the property, so I have never understood how some agents could justify their refusal to cooperate on an exclusive listing. But some of them have a regular practice of withholding cooperation from other brokers for varying degrees of time, always in their own selfish interest of trying to avoid having to split the commission with another broker.

I have observed that hoarding listings is self-defeating for the agents who practice it, since they usually do not sell the property themselves after all. The practice of hoarding listings also alienates other brokers who are not likely to forget the incidents, thus affecting future cooperative potential among the brokers concerned. So avoid the broker who is too selfish to give his full cooperation to other brokers at all times. He is not only selfish—he is not very objective and he will not handle the volume of business that is necessary in order to be productive for you.

SHOULD I BYPASS THE BROKER?

For a beginner, I would not advise dealing directly with another principal. There are too many things you do not know and, in the long run, you are apt to make a less profitable deal than you would have made had you used the services of a reputable broker. Or you could make a costly mistake by failing to include the necessary protective clauses in your purchase or sales agreement.

However, if the opportunity occurs and you want to try to handle the transaction yourself, be sure to get the advice of a competent real estate attorney—not just any attorney, which can almost be worse than none. Many attorneys who are not accustomed to real estate negotiations will unnecessarily complicate the transaction to the point where it may be difficult to get the deal through at all. I have worked with some attorneys who have been very practical in their approach and fully cognizant of the problems involved in negotiating. But I have seen more attorneys who tend to complicate the negotiations unnecessarily by adding all sorts of clauses designed to protect their client, when the clauses they were adding or changing meant essentially the same thing as the original form of the agreement.

A lot of restrictions and complicated demands put in a contract by a well-meaning attorney can make it difficult for you to get major concessions on important issues, such as the price of the property or other terms of the sale. You should always simplify your negotiations as much as possible, as long as you are protected.

Another problem with selling your own property is that it is very expensive to advertise. A broker can afford to advertise because he has other properties to sell to the prospect who responds to an ad, and in this way an ad can pay off for the broker. Also, it is a proved fact that the person who calls on an ad seldom buys the property he originally called on. So, the likely result of your trying to sell your own property is that you will run up a large advertising bill and still will not have sold your property. In order to find a buyer, you usually need a lot of prospects.

Negotiating directly with a buyer is very difficult and often impossible. The prospective buyer, if you succeed in getting one who is genuinely interested, will make you an offer. You will then refuse the offer, perhaps with an oral counteroffer. If the buyer finds that price unacceptable, the negotiations usually end there; whereas a competent broker

SELECTING AN AGENT 41

could have handled the negotiations in writing and worked out a compromise through various counteroffers and the use of some salesmanship.

Most people cannot sell their own properties, unless they are selling them below the market value. I have heard several sellers boasting how they sold their house to the first person who came by to look at it, etc. It's possible that they got a good price, but it is much more likely that the price was too low to begin with or that the statement was simply not true. Many brokers list their own properties with another office, or rely on their own sales staff to do the job.

The most singly effective tool you can employ when selling your own property is to act as though you are negotiating the sale between your partner (if you have someone who could be construed as a partner) and the buyer. In this manner, you can quietly play the part of the negotiator, always keeping your partner out of direct contact with the buyers. If the buyer's offer is not acceptable, you can use the excuse that your partner's approval is necessary and you will have to check it out with him, without committing yourself too much one way or the other. Tell the buyer that your partner will not consider anything that is not in writing, so it will be necessary to write up an official offer, accompanied by the standard good faith deposit of $100 to $1,000, depending on the price of the property and how much you can get out of the buyer.

Later, you go over the offer with your buyer and either accept it, giving a signed copy to the buyer, or write up your counteroffer and present it for the buyer's approval. If the buyer objects to your counteroffer, you can play the nice guy and say that your partner is the one who is holding out. In this way, you can often work out the price and terms to everyone's satisfaction. Whatever the buyer's reaction, get it in writing if possible. As long as there is activity in the negotiations, there is a chance an agreement can be reached. If you do not have considerable experience at writing sales agreements, you should have an attorney look it over before you sign anything final.

After all is said and done though, I would still recommend that most investors enlist the help of a reputable broker in transacting their real estate business. Unless the transaction has unusual complications, a good broker should be able to protect your interests adequately without the use of an attorney—though whether he would, in fact, actually protect your interests might be a different story. So, again, beware, but not to the point of getting discouraged.

ID # 5

How to Determine the Best Price

Obviously, the ideal solution in determining the best price to buy or sell a property would be to develop a foolproof formula which you could follow. But the solution is not that simple. All too often, I have seen the inaccuracy of organized appraisal methods as applied by professional appraisers representing banks, savings and loan associations, and other lenders. You could send any number of professional appraisers to some buildings and receive a wide range of appraised values. This situation is particularly true regarding the type of buildings I am proposing as the best targets for your investments.

I remember being involved, as a Realtor, in just such a situation. I showed a house, on the fringe of an exclusive area, to a friend who I thought would be interested in the house as a good opportunity to make a sizable profit with very little effort. The property was a small house consisting of five rooms. It had been occupied by one owner since it was built; she had become unable to care for it or herself and had moved in with relatives, putting the property up for sale.

The house was in very poor condition, to put it mildly. Obviously, nothing had been done to it since it was built approximately 30 years earlier. After looking at the house, which was priced at $31,000, my friend said he thought the asking price was too high. He liked the rehabilitation possibilities, however, and realized that it was close enough to a first class area to capitalize to some extent on the location. But in the end, he decided to make an offer of $23,000, apparently not caring much whether or not he got the house. When the counteroffer came back from the owner at $30,000, my friend said he was not interested. (Here I would like to point out that the house was listed with another broker and in multiple listing, so I did not know what sales action might be transpiring behind the scenes; and I did not have a fiduciary responsibility to the owner.) When I was sure my friend was no longer interested in the property, I put in my own offer at $30,000 and met all the other terms the owner had demanded in her counteroffer. I felt that I could have gotten some concessions through further negotiating, but I thought a house in the hand was worth two in the bush, and I was not willing to risk losing what I knew was an exceptional opportunity for the sake of trying to gain a thousand dollars or so in concessions.

After receiving the seller's ratification of my offer, I went to my bank for a loan. My banker assured me that there would be no difficulty in getting the customary 80 percent loan. However, when the banker called me back, about two weeks later, he seemed quite confused. He wanted to talk with me, he said. When I went to see him, he asked what was up. He said, "Brad, I know you're not a jerk and that you know what you are doing, but I can't figure why you are paying so much for that house."

I never did figure out exactly what he had on his mind, but I got a strong feeling that he thought I was phonying up the sales price of the house in order to get a large loan. (I have never used that illegal approach to investing, but it has been done and the lenders are sometimes justified in their suspicions.) My banker went on to say that their appraiser would appraise the house for a loan of $12,000, which was only 40 percent of the purchase price.

After considerable discussion with my banker, and he in turn with the appraiser, they finally offered me a loan of $13,500—still far short of any reasonable amount. Banks are notoriously conservative and because of the condition of the building I had been prepared for some hesitancy at giving me an 80 percent loan, but the final outcome was absurd. I could have gotten a better loan from the savings and loan associations, but by the time I got the bank commitment, escrow was ready to close and I did not have enough time left to go through the process of getting another loan commitment. As a result, I was forced to take the $13,500 loan and pay the balance in cash. However, I was able to get the bank to waive the normal pre-payment penalty clause so that I could pay off the loan at any time without penalty.

The outcome of this investment was that in a little more than six months time I sold the property for $48,000. Now why the exceptional value in that particular house? It was a large corner lot and I could tell from the dimensions that there was a possibility of splitting the lot, leaving the house, which was situated near the front corner, on its present site and splitting the lot 15 feet (minimum rear yard requirement for most residential corner sites in San Francisco) behind the house to create a new lot facing the other street, which happened to be the better of the two streets.

After checking with City Hall to make sure that the lot measurements were correctly stated on the multiple listing card, and inquiring as to the feasibility of splitting the lot, I was given reasonable assurance that it could be done. If it had turned out that I could not have split the lot, I could have backed out of the deal based on a loan contingency I had inserted in my offer. I did split the lot and sold the house for $26,500 and the vacant lot for $21,500, as a building site for a two-family dwelling. Both parcels sold shortly after I put them on the market, so the prices were obviously very reasonable. I am quite sure I could have gotten more, but I decided not to push the issue.

The only work I had done on the house was to spend $450 for a painter to steam off all the old, dreary wallpaper which covered all the walls and ceilings of the house. The effect of removing the wallpaper made the rooms appear much larger and more desirable than before, even though they showed many cracks and small holes which needed patching.

So the morals to this story are:

1. That you can't tell a house by its cover.
2. That you should not always rely on professional appraisers' opinions.
3. That good opportunities are available, even through the multiple listing service where the properties receive wide exposure. In fact, that particular property had been on the market almost a month before I first discovered it
4. Essentially, what it boils down to is that you must be able to appraise the property yourself in order to determine the fair market value—not relying on the opinion of anyone else. After having done that, you simply buy as low and sell as high as possible, to the extent practicable without jeopardizing a good deal.

APPRAISING THE SINGLE-FAMILY DWELLING

At the risk of over-simplification, I will give you some basic rules of thumb which, properly applied, will be helpful to you in determining what is the right price for the property you are considering buying or selling.

1. In a relatively new area with primarily new houses:

A. In this area, the method of appraisal is fairly simple and that is why, as I mentioned earlier, the opportunities for substantial profits from a fairly new single-family dwelling are limited. If it is easy for one person to determine the value, then the same applies to most other people, with the result that the asking and the selling prices are usually fairly close to the actual value.

A simple and effective method to help determine value is to compare the house with other recent sales in the same area. In comparing, however, you must take note of the differences in the properties, as well as the similarities—making a special effort to be objective, which is not always easy to do when you are a seller comparing your house with someone else's.

A good starting point is to take the square footage of the floor area, which can be obtained from your broker. The brokers estimate may be incorrect, however, and should be checked out if you are to rely heavily on this particular part of appraisal. If there has been a recent appraisal of the property, it may be possible to obtain the correct square footage from the appraising institution. Find out how many dollars per square foot the comparable houses sold for and use the same dollar figure to multiply by the square footage in the house you own or are considering, thus arriving at a figure we will refer to as your basic price.

Then, from the basic price, add or deduct for the difference in amenities between the buildings being compared. For example, if your house has a more modern and attractive kitchen or bathroom, then you should add a reasonable figure to the basic price of your house. The same principle should be applied to compensate for the difference in the number of bathrooms or bedrooms; or an extra room and bath on the garage or basement level; or other variations such as the general condition and appearance of the buildings; and the desirability of the different locations.

You would be surprised at how much higher a price an attractively decorated house will sell for than a house that shows poorly or only so-so. The arrangement and decorative appeal of the furniture and color schemes alone can make a big difference in the salability of a house. What it boils down to is that a house is worth as much as someone is willing to pay for it; and the willingness to loosen purse strings for a well-decorated house has been proved time and time again.

Also, watch for misplaced improvements, such as a very old house in the middle of a very modern neighborhood. An old house that sticks out like a sore thumb, even if it is an attractive sore thumb, will be worth a lot less in that neighborhood than it would be in an area consisting of similar buildings—where it would fit in and be appreciated.

2. In an area with a preponderance of old houses:

Old houses are mainly where it's at, as far as buying at a low price and selling at a high price. That is because older houses are more difficult to appraise, which should not bother you, once you learn to spot the good buys. The only time I have used the dollars per square foot as a guide to value in older buildings is to gauge the approximate amount of loan I can anticipate upon selling, when dealing with a house

HOW TO DETERMINE THE BEST PRICE

which has a relatively small total floor area. That is because the professional appraisers used by lenders do use the square footage as a part of their complicated method of arriving at the market value—but more often in a restrictive way only when the buildings are quite small, rather than to grant a large loan just because the building is quite large.

If reasonable square footage is not there, it may be difficult to get a large loan after you have remodeled the building and are selling it at a substantially higher price. Otherwise, as far as judging the value of old buildings in relation to the square footage, you can usually forget it. Some old buildings are so large that the cost of replacement, even after allowing for depreciation due to deferred maintenance and obsolescence, is much higher than the market value of the building. Of course, if a house is large, with large rooms, that is a definite asset and will affect the market value, as well as the appraisal—but not necessarily in direct relation to the size.

All of the above conditions must be taken into consideration, but the real key to value lies in factors such as floor plan, which is sometimes poorly arranged in old buildings; in the potential for change which would be appreciated by a large percentage of future prospective buyers; existing unusual features that need only to be accentuated; or possibly the removal or relocation of a wall to enlarge one of the rooms or otherwise create a feeling of open space. If the house appears dark and dreary, a good coat of white paint might brighten it up and perhaps visually enlarge a small room or hallway.

There are innumerable things to look for and evaluate, but perhaps the most important thing to look for is a selling feature that will catch the eye of prospective buyers. But be just as alert for bad features that may catch their eye too.

Also, try to be objective about the improvements you are considering and ask yourself whether each improvement will actually make enough of an impression on prospective buyers, or is it just something you personally fancy. If you are not objective here, you may be planning a lot of work and expense which might well be avoided. After all, the idea—and remember this always, even if you plan to live in the unit for a while—is to try to produce a product that will appeal to as many people as possible. The larger your market, the easier it will be to sell your product at a favorable price. Limit your market and you may have a very difficult time selling the property.

Make notes on what work you feel will be necessary in order to give the property an attractive appearance, both inside and out, limiting yourself, where possible, to work which will actually change the value of the property by being visually apparent to the buyer. Now put an estimated cost figure (rough) beside each item and add them up. When you reach this point, go through the appraisal guides I have given you, leaving out the square footage phase—you will have determined a rough value of the house as it stands.

Now compare this price with the price the house should sell for when the work is completed. Don't forget the costs of buying and selling. If you come up with a marginal profit figure, then be prepared to forget the house and go on to something else; or go over the house and your figures again to see if there are some changes which could be made; or consider whether you have projected your potential sales price too low. But do not go into a deal with anticipation of a very low profit margin. If you do, you may not make enough profit to make the whole thing worthwhile. Also, working with an anticipated narrow profit margin is leaving yourself open for possible loss. Whereas, if you have enough leeway, you will be able to absorb some mistake in your calculations or some unforeseen costly problem and still come out with a reasonable profit.

APPRAISING INCOME PROPERTY

Appraisal of income property is quite different from that of the single-family dwelling. Ownership of multiple-family dwellings, which I shall refer to as income property, is sometimes precipitated by pride of ownership, as is often the case with homes. But the predominant reasons for ownership of income property are: for tax deductions through the depreciation write-off it affords; for the benefit of the lower income tax rate afforded long term capital gains (when the property is sold); and for the sheer value of the income the property will produce, very often tax free. But when you get down to determining the market value of income property, an important question is: how much net income will the property generate?

What you will need is a simple method of determining the approximate market value of any given income property. There are several fairly simple rule-of-thumb methods used, such as "times gross" or 'times net" income. What those terms mean is that a particular building has a fair market value of 12 (or whatever figure is appropriate) times the gross annual income, because comparable buildings in comparable areas have recently sold for 12 (or whatever number) times their gross income. The same principle applies in using the "times net" income approach.

The appropriate gross or net multiplier that you should use will vary considerably from one area to another. For example, the gross multiplier used in Oakland, California, as a whole, has traditionally been higher than the one used in

San Francisco (with some exceptions I am sure), even though Oakland is just across the bay bridge from San Francisco. So, I repeat, employ caution in comparing properties in different areas, whether the area is in another city, or only a short distance away in the same city. Also, the better and more prestigious the area, the less return usually to be expected of the properties, for fairly obvious reasons.

If you are going to use the "times income" method of appraisal, obviously the "times net" method is more reliable, since the expenses of different buildings are not the same percentage of the gross income. Also, the method of analyzing the income from a building should vary depending on whether you are buying or selling the property.

1. Analyzing the income as a prospective buyer:

As a buyer you will be more concerned with how much income the building will produce—either in its present state, if you do not plan to improve the property; or in its improved state, if you plan substantial rehabilitation.

A. How much income will the building produce in its present state?

Take the gross annual income as represented by the seller or the seller's agent. Then consider whether that income is a reliable figure, based on the reasonable fair market value of the rental units. The existing rents are sometimes over-inflated which could cause difficulty in maintaining income, due to a high rate of turnover and vacancy.

On the other hand, if the existing rents appear to be low, how much more income could you get by increasing the rents? Consider any other factors which might justify an adjustment in the income, either up or down. Now adjust the alleged gross annual income by your calculated changes, adjusting either up or down as the situation warrants. From this figure, deduct a reasonable allowance for vacancy, and this will give you your adjusted gross annual income. Use a rule-of-thumb figure for the vacancy factor only if you are unable to arrive at a meaningful figure in some other manner.

In most instances, the vacancy factor of a building depends more on the management than on any other factor. For example, I have discovered from past experience that I can use a very low allowance for vacancy, except for the period when apartments must be kept vacant for remodeling—and even that can be kept to a minimum by effectively coordinating your work with your anticipated vacancies.

Now that you have the adjusted gross annual income, you are ready to calculate what you would expect your actual expenses to be. Starting with the alleged annual expenses, look over each expense to see if it is reasonably accurate, and look closely for any expenses that might have been omitted. Many expenses are often understated by the owners. The understatement of the insurance figure is sometimes considerable, particularly when the building has steam heat, which may require a separate and fairly costly policy on the boiler plant.

Check to see if each tenant has a separate utility meter. If not, be sure to take a close look at the alleged utility expenses. Probably, the most important expenses often omitted from the broker's statement are the expenses of management and janitorial services, and an allowance for maintenance. This is particularly true of fairly small apartment buildings where the owner may perform the duties himself.

Also, usually no mention is made of the potential post-sale reassessment by the tax assessor's office, since it is next to impossible to project accurately a reassessment in advance. But a fairly safe course for you to take, in the event that post-sale reassessments by the tax assessor are a common practice in your area, would be to figure on the possibility that the property might be reassessed upward to at least 50 percent to 75 percent of the difference between the existing assessment and the purchase price.

After you have adjusted the annual expense figures, deduct them from your adjusted gross annual income. This will give you the net annual income. Now, multiply the net annual income by the gross multiplier you have observed to be reasonable for the type of property and the location being considered. This should give you the approximate fair market value of the property.

B. How much income will the building produce after rehabilitation is completed?

The concern here is not how much income the present owner has been getting, but how much income can you anticipate after you have improved the property. The value to you is not in the present condition, since that is not how you plan to operate the building. Also, in case you plan to sell after you improve the property, the existing structure does not represent the same thing that you will be offering for sale.

So, to determine the adjusted gross income, forget about the alleged income and project the income you could anticipate after completing the work you expect to perform. From your projected income figures, deduct your allowance for vacancy and you will have your adjusted gross income. Calculate your expenses in much the same way as you would under "A" above, taking into consideration any changes in expenses that might be brought about by your rehabilitation efforts.

Total up your expense figures and deduct them from the adjusted gross annual income, which will give you the net annual income. Then multiply the net annual income by the gross multiplier, the same as in "A" above. The resultant figure should be the approximate fair market value of the building when you have completed your rehabilitation, not allowing for any change that might take place in the overall market conditions between the time you purchase the property and the time you complete your renovation. Hopefully, that factor will be positive, as it usually is based on the past performance of real estate values in general.

Now, deduct from the approximate fair market value the estimated cost of rehabilitation (arrived at by itemizing all cost items and then adding ten percent to cover miscellaneous contingency costs). The figure you now have should be the fair market value of the building to you—but not the price you will want to pay for it, since you must figure on a profit.

The application of the fair market value figures arrived at in both "A" and "B" above are essentially the same. The difference in the fair market value you have calculated and the price for which you can obtain the property will represent your potential profit. If the margin of profit you can anticipate by using the above figures is substantial, in relation to the total investment capital required, then the property may be a good investment. But before making a final decision, there are many other factors to consider and make allowance for, in order to determine the value.

2. Analyzing the income as a seller:

As a seller, arriving at the market value is less complicated. From the actual gross annual income, or the potential gross annual income you can anticipate without performing any work, deduct an allowance for vacancy, thus arriving at the adjusted gross annual income. Then deduct the actual annual expenses from the adjusted gross annual income, which will give you the net annual income. Now, multiply the net annual income by the appropriate gross multiplier. This should give you the approximate fair market value of the property, assuming that the gross income figure you have used is at, or near, the maximum potential that the property can produce. However, if the property has additional value based on its potential for rehabilitation, then you will need to follow much the same procedure as outlined under number "1.B." above, since the value is partially in potential which has not yet been realized.

Additional factors which affect the value of both single-family residences and income property are:

1. Is the present usage of the building or property tantamount to its highest and best use?
2. Does the property conform with local building and zoning ordinances? If not, what will be the cost of conforming?
3. Are the heating, plumbing (including a boiler for steam heat), and wiring facilities adequate?

4. Is the building structurally sound? A report by a licensed pest control operator may answer that question. However, there are instances, especially with large multiple-family dwellings, where an inspection by a structural engineer may be required—in face of evidence, or an appearance, that something critical may be wrong with the building, such as a leaning or sagging structure.

5. Are the room-sizes adequate—at least large enough so as not to be objectionable to the average persons who would be expected to inhabit the apartment or house, and for the price they would be expected to pay? Individual standards vary greatly, depending on what they are accustomed to and what they can afford.

6. Is the floor plan fairly good—as opposed to long, dark hallways; bedrooms located behind kitchens; other awkward or unattractive situations? These problems are more prevalent in buildings that have been converted from homes or flats, etc., to more units.

7. Is there any particular feature about the building that could be helpful in attracting a buyer? Or is there a particular feature that can't be changed which would discourage buyers at a substantially higher price?

8. Is the building over-improved for the area; namely is the price substantially above all other comparable, or similar, properties in the neighborhood? If so, it must be expected to sell for less than it would bring in a higher-priced area. Be cautious about buying the most expensive property in any area, or improv-

ing it to the extent that it becomes the most expensive in the area—it may be difficult to sell without a long wait for just the right buyer.

9. Is the building under-improved for the area? If so, you can expect it to sell for more than it would if it were in an area with comparably priced buildings.

10. Is the building a misplaced improvement?

11. If you are purchasing a building in a blighted area; an area not desirable to the masses; or even an area which might be questionable, be careful to adjust the price accordingly. Don't compare the price with more desirable areas.

12. How convenient are facilities for shopping and transportation and how important are they to the particular property?

13. If the property does not have parking space, it will be passed over by some buyers. Although off-street parking usually is not an all important consideration, an allowance should be made when adequate parking space is lacking.

14. What kind of financing is available? If the seller will carry the entire financing above your reasonable down payment, you can realize considerable savings on loan fees when buying, and on prepayment penalties when you sell, since loans carried by sellers do not usually contain loan fees or prepayment penalties. The interest rate you must pay, and other terms and conditions of the loan can have a large overall impact on your total costs. However, the interest rate is least important if you do not plan to keep the property very long.

An exception would be if you feel that the loan could be advantageously transferred to the new owner when you sell the property. The transfer of an existing loan may not be feasible, however, since your selling price would usually be considerably higher than the loan, thus requiring a larger down payment or the necessity of your carrying back a second loan for the buyer, unless a larger new loan is secured.

15. What is the demand for the particular type of property you are considering? A certain building style may be very popular in one neighborhood and just as unpopular in another. Then there are some styles that are uniformly popular and would fit in anywhere. Such buildings are fairly easy to spot, once you have looked around a bit, and they usually sell with a relatively low gross or net multiplier, because of the high demand.

16. What are the market conditions at the time you are considering buying? If the market is good and properties are selling readily, then you may have to pay more than you would in a slow market where most properties have been on the market for some time. Look for these trends, since they will give you a lot of insight into how hard you can bargain—whether you are the buyer or the seller.

17. Last, but not least important, what is the chance for improving the property without over-improving it for the area? And can the improvements be made primarily through decorative innovations? If so, the time, effort, and expenditure necessary to improve the property will be relatively small.

Before we leave the subject of buying and selling at the

right price, I want to stress a most important fact. Do not always try to purchase at the rock bottom price, and do not try to hold out for the absolute top price when you sell. Even though the idea is to buy low and sell high, any attempt to always achieve the ultimate in either direction will cause you more losses than gains, in the long run—to say nothing of the time lost in such efforts. If you always try to hold out for the best possible purchase price, you will lose many of the best opportunities to your competitors. If you always try to hold out for the top sales price, you will get stuck sitting on your property longer than it justifies.

The effects of trying to squeeze every last dime out of the property can be, and often are, counter-productive. For example, if you start with a price that is too high and unrealistic, the property may become shopworn, with the result that when you finally do get the price down to a realistic level, no one will seem very interested any more. The most costly factor is the time lost while waiting for just the right price. A quick sale for a reasonable price, which may net you a little less cash, will have the advantage of making it possible for you to put the money back to work again. So while you are holding out for another thousand dollars or so, you could make a lot more than that by putting your money to work in another investment. Plus the fact that, while you may eventually get the higher price you want, the price of other properties may have gone up just as much, or more, so you may have to pay more when you re-invest.

In any event, don't just decide on an arbitrary price and then try to stick to it in face of considerable opposition. Try to be realistic about how hard a bargain you should drive, for either the purchase or sale of the building, depending a great deal on just how important it is at the time to make the deal.

When buying, don't worry about how much the seller paid for the property—not even as a possible guide as to how low he will conceivably go on his price. Sometimes, sellers will fool you and sell at a loss. It depends on their motive for selling and on their mood at the time they receive an offer. Also, the price the seller paid may bear no resemblance to the fair market value. He may have overpaid for the property, or he may have gotten an exceptionally good deal, making it possible to sell the property again with a fair profit for himself, and still at a bargain price for the next buyer.

And don't pass up a property merely because it may have some negative features, just as you should not acquire one based on a single good feature. All of the good and bad must be weighed together. And remember that your objective has a great deal to do with finding properties that are available at a good price only because they have shortcomings that have turned the average prospect away, but which can be remedied.

6

Sources of Good Buys

There are systematic methods of finding good buys in real estate. The first rule is to specialize. Direct your interests toward a particular area and a particular kind of property such as single-family dwellings and residential income property, both of which can be handled together, since they are so closely related. But before we get further into the positive aspects of finding the right investment, I would like to mention some categories to be avoided.

AVOID UNIMPROVED LAND

Avoid unimproved land, especially as a beginner, and always if you are working with limited capital. There are a lot of good opportunities in land and a lot of fortunes have been made there, but they were usually made by individuals in high income brackets who could afford to purchase on speculation—just letting the land sit with the hope that it would become more valuable. Because they were usually purchasing with considerable leverage, as is the case with

SOURCES OF GOOD BUYS

most real estate, a relatively small increase in the value to the property would give a substantial return on the actual cash invested. During their waiting period, the investors were willing to make substantial mortgage and real estate tax payments out of their pockets, with little or no income from the land. But being in a high tax bracket, a good portion of the tax and interest deductions was absorbed by the resultant tax savings.

Land is usually slow to sell, and when it does sell the seller usually has to carry the financing for a large percentage of the purchase price, which ties up his funds for several years, at best. The good land investment is difficult to detect, and the waiting period before a substantial value increase can be anticipated could absorb the same amount of time it would have taken you to parley that same initial investment into a substantial fortune by investing in areas of real estate where a quick turnover could be effected.

For the land speculator, there is now the added problem of the environmental and open space freaks who can make almost any piece of property worthless for development purposes, almost at their whim. At best, anyone planning to develop land should anticipate a long and expensive hassle before gaining final approval of his plans.

AVOID COMMERCIAL PROPERTY

As a beginner, you should avoid commercial property, since it is generally slow to sell and just as slow to lease, with vacancies sometimes lasting for extended periods. Included in the commercial category to avoid are small hotels and guest houses (or residence clubs)—unless you want a full-time job of taking care of them, since they do require close supervision. And to go into this aspect of the real estate market on a large scale would require experience and know-how which most investors do not have. So, in short, stay away from them, unless you're well qualified to cope with the special problems inherent in the business.

FORGET "I COULD LIVE IN IT IF THINGS GET TOUGH"

Do not insist on finding property for investment purposes that you could live in "if things get tough." Unless you plan to live in the property for a long time, there is absolutely no reason why it need conform to the needs of your personal living standards and life style. I have seen prospective buyers pass up fantastic opportunities because they did not feel they would want to live there, even though they had no intention of ever living in the property. What you are looking for, or should be looking for if you want a good return on your investment, is a property you can purchase at a low price and then sell for a substantially higher price in a reasonable length of time, usually after making certain improvements. Why, then, should you tie yourself down with some foolish notion that you could live in the property "if things should get tough."

In the first place, in order to succeed in real estate investments, you will need to think positive. Second, I have never been able to understand how living in the property would necessarily be helpful to an owner, if things really got tough. A property can always be rented for some reasonable price, so you would collect some rent if you rented the property. And presumably, you would have either rent or house payments where you would live otherwise, so one offsets the other enough that you need not be obsessed with whether or not you could live in the property.

SOURCES OF GOOD BUYS

But let's suppose that things did "get tough." If things are tough, should you be so picky about where you live for a short period while you make arrangements for disposition of the property? Hopefully, and most likely, you will not need to be concerned with such things, but you should be prepared to make some sacrifices if necessary, at least until you get a substantial foothold in the business, or until you have enough funds to cover the expenses of a vacant property for a month or so. There is little likelihood that you would be unable to rent residential property for a period exceeding a month, if you have followed my instructions. But, again, if you want to go places in the real estate business, do not limit your investments by imposing impractical complications.

AVOID REAL ESTATE SYNDICATIONS

There are, sometimes, worthwhile investment opportunities in real estate syndications, but they are next to impossible to distinguish at the time you would be required to make your investment. And the best you could expect from real estate syndication ventures is a fair return on your money, which does not justify the risks involved.

In many ways, the real estate syndicate can be compared with the stock market's mutual funds. Some of them fare well, but all too often only when the market is booming, when the average person could have done just about as well by arbitrarily selecting various stocks. For a profit, the syndicates, as a whole, rely heavily on appreciation in the real estate market.

AVOID RESORT PROPERTIES AS INVESTMENTS

Most resort properties, and particularly those offered along with attractive inducements such as free travel and vacations, are almost always grossly over-priced. They are sold with sophisticated high-pressure techniques and can be made to seem very attractive, indeed. But the truth is that when the effect of the super sales pitch and the glamorous frills wear off, you are likely to find yourself with an overpriced piece of land which will be difficult to sell, for many years to come, at a price where you would get your money back. There must be some lucky souls who have been able to make a profit on resort subdivision purchases, but I have never met one who related that fact to me.

SO, HOW AND WHERE DO I FIND THE GOOD BUYS?

1. Of course you have the old faithful real estate ads where you can sometimes locate good buys that have just come on the market, but it requires following them regularly. Ads can be a problem because they make almost every property sound like the buy of a lifetime, but if you follow them regularly you will be able to recognize all the old ones after a while, even if they are reworded occasionally. That is surprisingly easy, since you will only be following a rather limited area.

2. Develop a good relationship with one or more active and knowledgeable brokers. They can be of invaluable service to you.

3. Attorneys can be a good source of good buys. They are very often consulted by property owners who are considering selling, some of whom have owned the property for many years; and the owners may have very little idea of current value, due to the effects of inflation over the years and the fact that they have been inactive in the real estate market

for some time. The attorneys are not usually acting in the capacity of recommending a sales price for the property, and even if they were, the chances are that they will have little knowledge of the value of any particular property. Remember, the attorney's business is law, not real estate appraisal. I have had bad experiences where attorneys advised their clients on property values and the advisability of certain investments. In the appraisal capacity, it is my experience that the attorney who ventures an opinion is more often wrong than not, usually giving a figure on the low side.

4. Banks and savings and loan institution foreclosures are an ideal source of low down-payment opportunities. They are also often very good buys, since the institutions are sometimes only concerned with recovering their investment and getting the property off their list of property holdings. Don't be hesitant to bargain with financial institutions, not only on the price, but also on the interest rate and the down payment. They will sometimes defer payments for a month or two if the property is not in rentable condition at the time you plan to take it over—or if there is an existing tenant who is not paying.

If the property is in a bad area and in really poor condition, do not hesitate to offer to purchase without a down payment—providing you have an excellent credit rating. You can sometimes work out the sale directly with the lender unless the property is listed with a broker. In any case, most brokers will not be familiar with what is available through these channels, so it would be best to contact the lenders first and if they have listed the property with a broker, they will let you know whom to contact.

5. Probate sales are sometimes worth investigating. But probate proceedings are awkward and restrictive—too much so to suit my taste. The information made available to buy-

ers is often sketchy. It is usually impossible to insert contingencies in your offer on probate sales without disqualifying the offer. Therefore, even the financing you may be able to obtain could be uncertain.

But the most discouraging problem for an investor who wants to keep his money working is that, even if he is successful in obtaining the original winning bid, the problem remains that he will not know for several weeks whether he will actually get the property, since anyone can raise the bid at the court proceedings, which are conducted two to three weeks after the original closing date for the purpose of confirming the sale. Probate sales entail too many uncertainties and are too time-consuming to make them attractive to ambitious investors who do not have the funds to keep their investments rolling while fooling with the probate deals on the side.

If, however, you do become involved in a probate sale, keep in mind the little-known fact that you may be able to get away with inserting contingencies in your offer. A lot depends on the competition. If it is a hot property and there is a lot of interest, then you can just forget about trying any negotiating. But I have had experience, representing a client, where an offer was accepted and confirmed in court with a low down payment and the seller carrying back a second loan. There were a couple of other contingencies in the deal which would not ordinarily have been accepted in a probate sale. This transaction took place during the midst of the tight money market when many probate offerings were left wanting for lack of buyer interest.

Ordinarily, a lot depends on the presiding attorney's attitude, but when there is no competition or your offer is better, overall, than other offers presented, then you may be able to get the owner to carry back a second loan or to go

SOURCES OF GOOD BUYS

along with some other requests not in keeping with normal probate proceedings. If you ask for these concessions in advance, however, you will most surely be told that it cannot be done.

6. Drive around in the area you have selected for investment and look for buildings that show signs of neglect, like a badly needed paint job, etc. When you find one, look up the owner (whose name usually can be obtained from the tax assessor's office, often by telephoning) and ask whether he would consider selling. If you do not wish to negotiate directly with the owner, then ask your broker to look into it for you, with the understanding that you will get first crack at the deal, if the owner wants to sell.

7. The Board of Permit Appeals, or the Abatement Appeals Board meetings (or your local equivalent agency) can provide a very lucrative source of investment opportunities. This source of business might be compared somewhat with that of the ambulance chaser, but it can, in effect, provide a valuable service to some distressed owners as well as an opportunity for the buyer.

Most properties which are the subject of hearings before these boards are in need of work required by the local building ordinances to bring them up to code. At the board meetings, the owners often relate their distress at having to comply with the complex, and sometimes confusing, work requirements. Very often, however, the improvements required are quite simple and can easily be remedied. An investor who approaches such an owner with the idea of purchasing the property in its present and as-is condition, will often find a most cooperative seller. Also, if you listen carefully at the hearing, and make notes on what work is unresolved, you will have a much better idea what you are tackling than you would with a good many properties presented for sale under normal circumstances.

8. One of the most important opportunities (and most often overlooked by the inexperienced investor) in the real estate field is the tremendous advantage available to the buyer when there is a really severe buyer's market (when properties are very slow to sell and the buyer can dictate the terms, because the seller knows he may not get another offer for a long time).

I remember times (approximately 1966 to 1970) when a good percentage of the properties listed for sale were not even attracting lookers. Many properties stayed on the market for two to three years without even so much as one offer to purchase. And many of them were owned by people who genuinely wanted to sell. During that period, an investor who was willing to make an offer substantially under the asking price often got himself an acceptance and a good buy. Some sellers were so tired of waiting for an offer that they were most agreeable indeed.

I did not personally take advantage of this situation the way I could have, since it did not fit in with my plans of limited expansion. But I was able to prosper as a broker during this period, when many real estate brokers and investors alike were going out of business—very often broke—while others held down night jobs in order to keep their real estate office doors open during the day. So, the key is to adjust to the times. What might seem like basically bad times may be the best times of all, depending on your position and your objective, of course. So be alert to opportunities opened up by the change in the market.

9. Through whatever source it comes to your attention, be alert to the opportunities available in a small and/or old run-down building on a large lot. The owner may be willing

SOURCES OF GOOD BUYS

to sell based on the size and condition of the building, when the actual value may be in the lot. The ideal lot of this type is the corner, since it usually holds the key to access from two streets, plus the advantage of controlling any substantial development of the adjoining lots. Corner lots are prime targets for large buildings because the zoning ordinance allows for covering a larger portion of the corner lot, plus the advantage of having more sides open to light and air.

But if you can't get the corner, sometimes acquisition of the lot next to, or near, the corner will enable you to control further development of the corner parcel. This type of application can be especially rewarding when the lot in question is located within one to four blocks of an impending rapid transit station, or any other development which could spark unusual development interest in the area.

One of the problems of this approach to investing is that it can sometimes be a long waiting game, which may be all right if you can keep your cash investment to a minimum and the property will pay its own way while you are waiting. Don't forget to check the zoning restrictions on the parcel before you buy—and be alert to any proposed changes for re-zoning the area.

Another note of caution. Anticipated large scale developments which are likely to change the character of an area sometimes run many years behind their scheduled completion. In such cases, where you may have to hold the property for a long time, invest as little capital as possible so that your return on the investment will still be high, due to the advantages of substantial leverage.

The advantage of leverage works something like this. Suppose the purchase price is $100,000 and you invest a total of $10,000 (a good leverage position), with a loan or loans totaling $90,000. After a wait of, say four years, you sell the property for $140,000 because someone wants the site for a large building. Your percentage return on your investment would be 400%, or 100% average for each year that the investment was held—and you would have built up an equity in the monthly payments, and you no doubt would have realized tax deductions during the four-year period you were holding the property.

It is unlikely—though possible—that you would have any cash flow to speak of, what with a low down payment and the large debt service. Of course you are taking a chance that nothing constructive will develop on such an investment, but if you choose several, and choose wisely, one or more of them will come through and will make up for the lack of activity in the others. And even the ones that don't work out as hoped should yield a reasonable profit in the long run.

10. Other helpful hints to assist in getting good buys.

   A. Don't shy away from a property just because the tenants are not paying their rent. I have seen many properties sold at low prices by discouraged owners, simply because the tenants would neither move nor pay the rent. There are solutions to evicting tenants, so just make the necessary allowance for the costs involved. And uncooperative tenants can often be handled effectively with nothing more than persistent and persuasive prodding. Sometimes it is only a matter of diplomacy and communicating with the problem tenants to get to the bottom of the difficulty. It may be that they only want some minor repairs taken care of, or some such thing.

   B. Don't give up just because you have a difficult and unyielding seller. Try to think of concessions you can negotiate to your advantage while giving in to the

SOURCES OF GOOD BUYS

seller's particular demands. Some sellers get so hung up on an issue that they fail to see the pitfalls inherent in their actions.

C. Watch for sagging floors or slanting walls, or an excess number or size of wall cracks. These may be the result of natural and quite harmless settlement, but they may also be warning signals of the existence of some sort of foundation or structural problems. One simple, often effective, way to detect the lack of proper foundation support in any particular part of a building is to give an abrupt shove downward with your heels to see how much the building shakes or vibrates. If proper foundation support is lacking, then you will probably get some telling response to such a jolt.

D. Before firmly committing yourself to buying a property, take the time to check with the local government planning department to see if there is any planned or proposed development in that area—such as government housing projects, which lower the property value of the surrounding area. Or check to see whether the property is in any sort of government-enforced development or renewal area, which could result in costly work requirements, indefinite delays, and the shutoff of virtually all conventional financing markets for the area concerned. Any of these could cause difficulty and delay in selling the property.

E. Check out the property thoroughly. Don't just breeze through. To check the water pressure, turn on a couple of water faucets and then flush the toilet while they are running. If the water pressure changes too much, it could be an indication that the water pipes need replacing, or that the building needs new water service from the meter, due to corrosion-plugged pipes.

F. Don't be in too much of a rush to buy. Take the necessary time and precautions to make sure that you know what you are getting into—though at the same time try to avoid needless delays which could cause you to lose out on good deals. But, in the end, if the delay seems necessary, just remember that there will be other opportunities. Good buys are everywhere—you need only to learn how to recognize them.

7

Profit Advantages of Condominiums

The advantages of the condominium apartment over that of the co-op are such that I will dwell exclusively on the condominium concept of apartment ownership. Contrary to the co-op, which amounts to joint ownership under one deed, with one loan, etc., each condominium unit may be bought, sold, taxed, and mortgaged independently of the others. The individual owners share ownership of the common elements of the property, such as the roof, yard, basement, elevator, and so forth. Each owner of a condominium participates in stock ownership in a non-profit corporation formed to provide for care and maintenance of the common areas. Each owner is obligated to share the expense of maintaining the common areas, usually paid in monthly assessments on each apartment in relation to the respective percentage ownership in the total project.

The condominium owner has the advantage of tax deductions for the interest and taxes paid on the property—as well as the advantage of depreciation, in the event the apartment can qualify as an investment for tax purposes. There is also the advantage of a low tax liability on the land, since it is shared by all owners. The owner of a condominium unit may be required to obtain approval of the other owners before making any substantial structural alteration or change in decorating, but this and other restrictions depend on the deed restrictions as arranged by the developer of the project.

DANGERS OF OVER-EXPANSION

The condominium concept of home ownership has caught on in the past few years to the extent that it has reached the contagion stage. The pace of new condominium construction has been so rapid in the past few years that in many areas it has, along with other rapid land development, outstripped the capacity of local sewage and water treatment facilities. This has recently led some communities to take steps to halt growth by adopting "no growth" policies.

In some areas the pollution control departments have placed moratoriums on development until further studies can be made, or until public facilities can be improved or expanded. In fact, such problems—plus the growing trend of many communities toward restricted growth, along with the help of conservationist and environmentalist protection agencies—are starting to put a damper on interest in potential new developments, thus opening up a whole new field of investment opportunities through conversion of existing apartment buildings into condominium apartments.

However, since the ban on further construction does not affect work already in progress, an over-built situation is likely to occur in many areas—especially since many builders will foresee the possibility of the ban and thus rush a flood of building permits through ahead of it. What this does is to intensify an already mushrooming production situation to the point where an over-supply is likely to occur, at least temporarily. New construction under these permits will, however, in most cases, be completed within one to two years after the ban on further construction has been imposed.

THE CLUSTER CONCEPT

There is some controversy as to whether the cluster concept of condominium development is more desirable than well-spaced individual housing, but the cluster approach is generally accepted as the lesser of the evils inherent in the large scale development of land. As many people see it, the condominium is a partial answer to the growing high cost of land.

Persistent inflation in land, materials, and labor for construction costs, has given the cluster concept of development a big push. It is perhaps the best solution presently available for efficient and practical land planning and development. By clustering housing units, more open space can be provided. At the same time, a cluster can be designed and constructed to produce the appearance of one large single-family dwelling, which tends, to some extent, to satisfy the proponents of more open space. The cluster approach also tends to placate planners who have objected to traditional subdivision developments.

The high density that the condominium concept of construction allows saves on practically all cost factors, including centralized plumbing, common sewer and utility hookups, common walls, roofs, foundations, and so on. The joint ownership of common areas relieves the owner of general exterior maintenance and yard work, the cost of which can run from a very low of $20 per month on some low maintenance and inexpensive projects to $50 and up on more luxurious apartments.

The fourplex condominium

While there are condominium projects of up to 1000 units, the fourplex unit has become the most widely exploited concept of cluster housing. The fourplex may be sold as an investment to an owner who wants to live in one unit and rent out the other three. However, attempts to sell the projects on this basis have run into the same buyer resistance that the conventional four-unit building has encountered. Most home owners do not like the idea of so many renters at their doorstep; but on other merits the fourplex has really caught on. In some areas, three out of every four new "single-family" housing units are actually fourplex condominiums.

Some builders have been able to provide condominium apartments for the large market of buyers looking for a home under $20,000. This is accomplished by eliminating a lot of the costly frills that are included in most homes, and by constructing more units per acre than would be possible with single-family dwellings. It has the advantage of providing a unit for many owners who would otherwise be unable to purchase a home. On the average, the cost per unit is approximately 20 percent less than the cost of comparable detached single-family dwellings.

Financing the condominium project

In financing condominium projects, the down payment is often a larger percentage of the total purchase price than is the case with detached single-family dwellings. This is not always true, however. Apartments are sometimes financed with as little as five percent down. FHA and VA financing are often available, though conventional lenders are the prime source of financing for this market.

FHA-and VA-insured financing present basically the same obstacles, such as high-discount loan fees and time-consuming delays, that plague the conventional housing market and have, in recent years, led to less and less use of these sources. On either conventional or government-insured mortgages which extend for 30 years, monthly payments are sometimes less than rent in comparable housing.

NO QUICK PROFIT IN A NEW CONDOMINIUM

It is my feeling that purchasing a newly-constructed condominium apartment as an investment, with anticipation of making a large profit, would be a mistake—the same as expecting to turn a quick profit by purchasing new housing of any type. Though some projects will enjoy a substantial increase in value due to unusual demand for the particular location or design, it would be next to impossible to pick the few which would have that type of success.

WHERE ARE THE GOOD BUYS?

There are, however, attractive opportunities in condominium development which can be exploited by the average investor who is well-informed about the real estate market as a whole. But many special considerations must be taken into account in developing condominiums projects which are, in effect, subdivisions requiring the filing of a subdivision map outlining the exact lines of division between the individual apartments and the common areas—as well as complying with other normal subdivision requirements—with the exception that the division of four or fewer units would not usually require compliance with the Department of Real Estate Subdivision Map Act. As a rule, the division of either improved or unimproved land into four or fewer units is regulated by the local planning commission only. Some communities refer to four-unit land divisions as "minor subdivisions" and most communities would have considerably less rigid restrictions than those required by a subdivision creating five or more parcels. Although either form of subdivision is by no means a simple undertaking, it is not as difficult as it might at first seem.

Used units in older condominiums

The only area where the average investor should look for substantial gains in the buying and selling of condominium apartments is in existing used units in older buildings. To remodel or redecorate an existing condominium unit you should employ much the same principles outlined for other residential property that are owner-occupied. Many older condominiums were established at a time when construction costs were low, and if enough time has lapsed, some of them will have become worn and tired looking, or a bit outdated. So the objective should be to find one in a good area, with spacious rooms and a potential for upgrading. But you must keep in mind that the exterior and the common entrance must be attractive enough to be accepted by potential buyers—once you are ready to sell the rehabilitated apartment—since you most likely will not have the right to make improvements to that portion of the property. But you might be able to use your influence, as one of the owners, to persuade the other members to go along with voting for redecorating the exterior, the entrance, or other common areas, where improvement would be in the best interest of all owners.

Since condominium living is in closer proximity than is the case with detached single-family dwellings, it is more important to consider the caliber of the other occupants. If a revamping of the common area is necessary in order to carry through with profitable rehabilitation and sale of a particular unit, a poll of the other owners should give you a good indication as to what kind of opposition you can expect to encounter. This could presumably be done before committing yourself to a firm purchase contract.

Converting apartment buildings

For the experienced investor, the best opportunities for gain in the field of condominiums lie in the prospect of converting apartment buildings into condominium apartments. Opportunities along this line have been greatly enhanced, during the past year or so, as a direct result of "no growth," or controlled growth, policies that have been implemented. Since the conversion of an existing apartment into a condominium unit does not actually add to the existing housing supply, it is less objectionable than the construction of new units. Lower density zoning is abounding in suburban areas throughout the nation. Also, opponents to further expansion of housing in many areas have devised ingenious, though often seemingly illegal, methods of blocking new land development. The effect of the growing objections to new development is that a good percentage of the demand for independent housing units must now come from the existing supply—and the most convenient and pliable source of housing for individual ownership is in converting regular apartment buildings into condominium apartments.

APPEALING ASPECTS—
WHO BUYS CONDOMINIUMS?

One of the most appealing aspects of condominium ownership is the fact that the maintenance and upkeep of the building and surrounding common areas are taken care of, thus relieving the owner of the usual ownership responsibilities. This can be especially appealing to individuals who are away from home a great deal for either business or personal reasons. So it is important to keep in mind, when considering a potential investment for conversion purposes, the prospects of meeting the needs and desires of future owners.

For example, buyers of condominium apartments fall into three basic categories: the old, the middle-aged, and the young. Young people who cannot afford a single-family home, or who do not want the responsibility that goes along with it, are prime prospects. They may consider it only as a temporary arrangement until they can build up an equity for the more costly purchase of a detached home, perhaps also after more children necessitate an expansion. Middle-aged couples are often anxious to rid themselves of the cost and bother of maintaining a large house once their children have grown up and gone off to college or on their own.

Attract the senior citizens

Perhaps the largest group of the three is the older group. The apartment that would appeal to older people must often be more specialized. Many older people like the flexibility that apartment ownership affords so they can use the apartment for a few months out of the year, while having it rented out for a portion of the year to help defer expenses and to provide a tax deduction through depreciation. In that event, some sort of rental service would be required as a part of the project operation. Many older people can afford and are willing to pay for extra frills and recreational facilities, such as pools, clubhouses, and even golf courses. Many of them also follow the sun, and this group is prone to condominium ownership.

So be alert to the special catering that will be necessary in order to tap a large segment of the older group. Ideally, for this market, a club-like atmosphere should be created; for what they will want is more than just a home or an investment. Many of them must be convinced that owning a condominium apartment is preferable to spending several months in a local hotel or motel, or perhaps a high-rent apartment or home, while at the same time providing a situation that is not a great deal more expensive.

Good rentals make good condominiums

Generally, the property most suited to conversion is one which has proved to be a desirable rental. If the property is fairly new or in excellent condition, then the class of people you can expect to sell the apartments to will usually come from approximately the same level as that of the existing tenants. In fact, under reasonable conditions you should be able to sell about 30 percent of the apartments to the existing tenants, particularly if you can arrange a sale price and financing that will provide for monthly payments approximately equal to the rental value of the unit.

However, with older buildings where remodeling is necessary, or where substantial landscaping and improvement additions or redecorating would be required, the tenant makeup would probably change so much that most of the existing tenants would not desire, or qualify for, apartment ownership. With this type of property, you would need to decide which group you could best satisfy with the existing amenities or with practical additions or alterations.

The setting must catch the eye

Most condominium projects should have an attractive exterior and entry approach. If the building consists of more than two stories, it should have an elevator. And in the case of luxury units, the exterior should be impressive as well—and the prestigious appeal of the area would be very important. In tall buildings, ideally, but of course by no means necessarily, each unit would cover the entire floor on which it is located, making for more privacy and a feeling more like that of a single-family home. In the luxury field, the rooms must be spacious, with ample light and open exposure, and with a pleasant outlook. If available, an appealing view could also add several thousand dollars to the value of some apartments, and would certainly enhance the value of any unit. Sometimes, the potential of a view existed but was not exploited at the time the building was originally constructed, since views have not always been in vogue. Perhaps, the features most in demand by buyers of suburban condominium units, at all levels, are swimming pools and tennis courts.

CONVERSION POINTERS

Basically, most of the same principles for decorating and remodeling would apply to condominium apartments as for other homes and residential investment property, as outlined in detail in Chapter 13. I will not attempt to give a complete rundown on the semantics of converting regular apartments to condominiums, since the requirements are far too complex and variable under state and local ordinances, but the following pointers will assist in qualifying properties which could be considered for profitable conversion:

1. Generally speaking, after selecting the property you feel would be desirable for conversion, you should secure an option to purchase the property, subject to obtaining the necessary permits for conversion. The option period should be

PROFIT ADVANTAGES OF CONDOMINIUMS

for as long as six to eight months, if possible, and at least three months, since it could easily take that long to get through the red tape you would encounter. It would probably be necessary to advance some option money to the seller of the project, which would be forfeited in the event you abandoned the idea of purchasing.

It is quite possible, however, to get a conditional sales contract, rather than an outright option. They amount to basically the same thing except that under the conditional sales contract you would not normally forfeit your deposit in the event the contingencies could not be satisfied. However, before you go into a project of this type, you should have reasonable assurance that you can accomplish your goal, in which case you should be willing to put up some reasonable option money, if necessary.

2. Before going into a conversion project, you should make a thorough assessment of the market demand and ask yourself whether that demand is likely to hold up for the length of time it would take to complete the subdivision requirements. Additional time could be required to sell the apartments, since the sale or lease of any part of a subdivision is prohibited by law until a final map is filed and recorded, in full compliance with the subdivision map act. In fact, in most areas there will be an additional requirement that a minimum percentage of the apartments be sold before title can be transferred. This is done to protect the unwary individual purchaser in case only a few units are sold and the developer decides to rent the larger portion of the units. Such a situation would lower the market value of the units already sold. Also, the lender will almost surely require that a certain percentage of the units be sold before financing can be arranged for sale of the individual apartments. In most cases, the lender will not finance the sale of any of the apartments

until at least 51 percent, and sometimes more, have been sold, in order to insure against the developer abandoning the idea of selling the majority of the units.

While it is not permissible under most or all subdivision map acts to enter into a sales agreement on condominium apartments until the map act requirements have been satisfied, it may be possible to take an "advance reservation" on individual apartments. The reservation is binding on the seller but not on the buyer. By doing this, buyers can be lined up so that the required 50 percent to 60 percent ownership participation may be satisfied immediately upon obtaining approval to sell the units.

3. To avoid complications, at the time of securing the original loan on the building to be converted, you should have a release clause in the mortgage agreement which will provide that the lender give partial reconveyance after a certain percentage of the apartments are sold. Failure to arrange a release clause, prior to going into the subdivision, could result in the existing lender requiring that the entire loan be paid off before reconveying any part of the property. For many investors, such a requirement would create a real crisis.

The existing lender will usually require that at least 51 percent of the apartments be sold before reconveying title to any of them. The lenders who finance the sale of the individual apartments will have comparable requirements. What these requirements do is to necessitate the closing of escrow on at least 51 percent of the sales simultaneously. This could conceivably present some problems in the event that selling the apartments turned out to be a slow process. If possible, you should also make advance arrangements with the original lender for transferring a reasonable portion of the loan to the buyers of the newly-converted apartments, along with the partial reconveyance of the deed. A firm commitment of such arrangements may be difficult to arrange, but you could probably reach some sort of understanding which would save you all, or part, of the pre-payment penalty on the portion of the loan to be paid off at the time of each reconveyance.

4. You should check out the attitude of the local planning staff whose approval you would need in order to complete the project, since planning commissions have considerable leverage in administering local subdivision ordinances. Requirements will also vary because converting existing properties into condominium projects is a relatively new field and some officials will be reluctant to exercise discretion. Some planning departments will go as far as requiring control over the maintenance provisions set up to cover the care of the common areas. Some will not want common walls joining the units, which may sometimes be eliminated by constructing a fake wall in one of each two adjoining units.

Then there are some planners who will make few demands over and above what they would make in requiring that regular apartment buildings be brought up to code. What it all boils down to, is that unless you have the reasonable cooperation of the local planning department, you should look for another community, where you would encounter less resistance, for your investment.

5. Make sure that the existing zoning of the building site will permit rebuilding the structure in the event it were to be destroyed by fire—if it does not, then the local planning department may refuse to grant permission for the subdivision. Most planners take a protective attitude toward the future owners of projects they are considering for approval. One planner explained his attitude by saying that he wanted to protect innocent little-old-ladies from purchasing a con-

verted apartment where some major problem could develop.

6. Be alert to the fact that, in many cases, condominium subdivision will necessitate more strict adherence to the building code than would be the case if the building were left as an apartment building—even though the code requirements might be essentially the same.

7. In projecting the total costs of a project to be weighed against the total market value of the apartments, be sure to include such costs as the surveyor's fee, the engineer's fee for drawing up the map and plans outlining the division of the individual apartments and the common area, the developer's or attorney's fee for drawing up the covenants and restrictions, and fees for state and local permits—the total sum of which could run roughly $6,000 for a 15-to-20-unit project. The costs would be proportionately less for smaller projects, with a possible minimum of around $2,000 for a simple division.

YOUR FIRST INVESTMENT— MAKE IT A SMALL ONE

As always, in going into a new field where you may be dealing with unknown quantities, your first investment in a condominium subdivision should be a small one. You should either pick a four-unit building for the first project, or go into a larger project with a partner, or partners, who have had considerable experience. The largest market for condominium apartments is in the $20,000 to $40,000 price range, and it would be advisable to stay within that range until you have enough experience to decide whether to tackle the more limited markets. But in any case, do not attempt a condominium subdivision unless you have had considerable experience and success in less-complicated real estate investmnts, and until you have a substantial cash reserve for contingency factors.

Finally, be sure to get the advice of counsel who has had local first-hand experience with condominium subdivisions, though such persons are not easy to find. First-hand experience is essential at this time because, although most local government entities follow the dictates of the Department of Real Estate Subdivision Map Act and the local city and county subdivision ordinances, many planners and inspectors of the projects do not yet have a clearly-defined understanding as to the requirements of a condominium subdivision. This situation is aggravated by the fact that, due to the intricate nature of some conversions, new questions have been raised that have not yet been answered.

8

Preparing Your Property for Sale

The property which will sell first and for the best price is the one which shows good. I have seen many brokers, and indeed have done it myself, get out and sweep, or hose down, the front walk of a house they are marketing, when the owner has left it looking like an eyesore.

APPEARANCES COUNT

To get the best reception from the prospective buyers, you should make the house as presentable as you possibly can. An unkempt house is no asset to selling. If someone told you he would give you a thousand dollars, or perhaps more, if you would get busy and wash those dirty windows, sweep or hose down the front walk, and even that of your neighbors if necessary, clean or replace those dirty or worn out drapes, etc. . . ., would you do it? Sure you would. And that's about what it amounts to when you make your house presentable. You'll get a better price and a lot sooner.

I know of some people who have even gone so far as to

go out and rent paintings to hang on the walls for a month or so while showing their house for sale. If you don't already have some nice paintings or other articles with which to decorate your house, you might consider doing the same thing. The addition of a group of attractive and properly-arranged paintings can do wonders for the appeal of a house.

AVOID UNNECESSARY COSTS

Sometimes there are fairly costly items that need fixing in order to make a house show to its best advantage. If this be the case, and you can afford the improvement, it may be well worthwhile. But before you act, consider the cost of the project and just what additional appeal it will add to the house, if any. All too often, owners make costly changes which make little or no difference in the salability of the house.

In some cases, the poor souls actually spend a lot of time, effort, and money on some change that is not appreciated by prospective buyers who would have preferred the house in its original condition. So, try to be objective and don't change anything unless you are fairly sure it will appeal to the majority of likely buyers. The removal of an eyesore can be an invaluable asset to assist in the sale of your house, but changes that will not be appreciated by the majority of prospective buyers can be a disaster.

LIMIT YOUR REMODELING

Nobody wants to pay what he assumes is a higher price due to remodeling, when he does not appreciate the work that was done and feels that it would need to be done over.

I have heard the saying so many times, "I don't want to pay that price for this building, when I'll have to do all the work over again." This comment is most often inspired by shoddy workmanship. Be sure, in whatever changes you attempt, that the quality of your workmanship is fairly good. Poor workmanship stands out like a sore thumb and will make any property almost impossible to sell at a reasonable price.

Don't lose sight of your objective. You want to produce a product that will appeal to others. Hopefully, your tastes and theirs will coincide, but if there is a reasonable chance that they may not, then perhaps you should not make the change. Or you could seek the advice of a professional decorator. The money might be well spent, but don't be persuaded to go overboard. Many decorators get carried away and spend more money than the investment possibilities warrant, even when it is their own money they are spending. So, if you consult with a decorator, just take the best and least expensive suggestions and let the rest go. If you use restraint, a decorator's ideas can be most helpful.

9

Getting Involved with a Partner

I have not been too keen on partnerships for the purpose of developing real estate. I have always felt that a partnership would only handicap me, primarily by restricting the application of the most effective and expeditious treatment of investments. I have owned buildings in partnership, but primarily during the early stages of my career when it would have been difficult to handle a purchase on my own.

A SILENT PARTNER IS BEST

If you choose to enlist a partner, for whatever reason, be certain that you have carefully considered the potential hazards of such a move. If you have enough confidence in your own judgment and ability to develop the property to its best potential, then the ideal partner for you would be one who is more or less a silent partner—one who would let you make all the major decisions, such as what type of improvements you intend to undertake, when to sell, and at what price, etc. If you get a partner who is not too knowledgeable or practical, but who still wants to have his say in the handling of the property, it can be a problem.

I could cite many examples of partnership participation where one or the other did not have good judgment regarding the improvements that should be undertaken, usually insisting on elaborate, costly, and time-consuming remodeling which could not be justified on the basis of the potential selling price. And, too, there is always the problem of who is doing the most work or putting in the most effort.

If you can get an easy-going, reasonable, and fairly intelligent person for a partnership venture, then I would say go ahead if you need the additional capital in order to handle the investment, or if you need help in qualifying for financing.

On the other hand, if you do not feel secure enough in your judgment to go it alone, then look for a partner who is knowledgeable and capable of carrying the ball. Two uncertain investors in the same project can be worse than two know-it-alls.

Then, too, there is always the possibility that two heads can be better than one. But don't count on it, because it will not prove true in all cases—it depends entirely on the heads.

JOINT OWNERSHIP

Taking title under joint ownership can be a little tricky, so make sure you know how you want to hold title. See the definitions at the end of the book for an explanation of Joint Tenancy and Tenancy in Common. It would be advisable to consult with an attorney or the title insurance company when there is any doubt as to how title should be held. It can get especially complicated between husband and wife, as a result of community property laws, etc.

GETTING INVOLVED WITH A PARTNER

Before leaving the subject of partnership participation in real estate investments, I would like to mention an experience I had on one of the few occasions when I invested along with a partner, and the only time I had more than one partner. Fortunately both partners were fairly easy-going individuals—otherwise it could have been a real disaster.

One of the partners was supposed to live in one of the three units rent free, in exchange for painting and decorating that unit. The major work, which consisted of a completely new bathroom and some remodeling in the kitchen, was done mostly by outside help. The live-in partner was only supposed to do some light patching and painting and a small amount of wallpapering in one room. This was to have been done in about three-months time, in exchange for free rent for the same amount of time. Then the property was to be put up for sale.

I forget exactly how long the partner lived there rent free, but it was the better part of a year. And not only did his doing the work himself not save us money, it cost more in materials and supplies than it would have cost to hire a painter, to say nothing of the loss of time and income we suffered as a result of his approach to the whole affair. He was a perfectionist personified. He was supposed only to patch lightly and paint, but instead of doing that, which would have been quite adequate, he steamed all the wallpaper off the walls. That would have been all right for a place he planned to keep and live in for a long time, but for a quick turnover on a property it was unthinkable, since the wallpaper had already been painted over several times in the past and would have looked fine with a good coat of paint.

If you have never steamed wallpaper off a 70-year-old Victorian house, take my advice and don't try it unless it is a must. Once the paper is off, all the cracks and small holes that have accumulated over the years really show up, and the necessary patching takes forever. Anyway, after he got the wallpaper off we discovered he did not know how to patch. So the other partner and I went in and showed him how to do it, and in the process completed the patching and painting of one room. Afterward, the live-in partner decided the patching was not perfect, so he started all over again, patching and sanding and repainting. He did the whole unit in roughly the same manner.

In the dining-room, he put up wallpaper from end to end, and then, again deciding that it was not perfect, he wallpapered it over again. The experience with his grouting the tile around the new bathtub was similar. The grouting job, which would normally have required a few hours at most, took him over a week. It was incredible, and his re-doing everything two or three times finally caused the third partner to refuse to have anything to do with the property. I had to smooth things out in order to avoid a serious conflict.

Fortunately the live-in partner was an exceptionally nice person, and while his approach to refurbishing the property was absurd, he believed in what he was doing. And as bad as it was to contend with and for all the lost time and money, I would prefer his approach to shoddy workmanship. At least when the property was ready for sale, we did not encounter resistance to the workmanship.

It has been interesting over the years to watch the progress of the individual mentioned above. One would think that with practice he would have learned to get a little more done without such to-do. But, if anything, he got worse, it seems; probably because he has been on his own with subsequent investments, with no one to push him. The last I heard he was still working on a very small three-room apartment (a basement or garden apartment), doing some minor remodeling. The work had been in progress well over a year and it still was not ready to rent. He could have gotten the work done by an expensive contractor and rented the apartment a month after starting the remodeling, and the proceeds from the rent would have paid the contractor long before the apartment was completed by the owner.

So, while good workmanship is important, you cannot be a perfectionist when remodeling property for rent or a quick sale, if you expect to make a reasonable profit in a reasonable length of time. If you discover that it takes you an unusually long time to get the work done, you will almost surely come out ahead financially by hiring a contractor to do the work—plus the advantage of not having to slave over the project for an eternity. And if you plan to turn the investment over and go on to something else, the time saved will be invaluable. If you want to prosper with real estate investments, you must take a reasonable approach to the handling of your acquisitions.

If you want a partner, choose carefully and then be prepared for some trying moments.

10

Property Management

Successful management is one of the major keys to success in dealing with residential income property. There are some people who manage their property so badly that, eventually, they throw up their hands in despair and sell out, sometimes at a loss because of the poor state of the property after having been mis-managed.

DON'T IGNORE TENANT COMPLAINTS

It does not pay to neglect the serious needs of tenants. Failure to heed their complaints will result in high turnover, which is time-consuming and costly, since most vacancies necessitate some redecorating, even if only touching up, plus correcting the disparity that caused the trouble in the first place. So keep your tenants happy as long as their requests are reasonable. The objective of successful management is to minimize the time and effort involved in dealing with each property, while at the same time keeping expenses down and getting the maximum return that is practical under the prevailing circumstances.

FIND THE RIGHT MANAGER

With a building which has sufficient dwelling units to justify a resident manager, the problem is primarily that of finding the right manager. This may take some time, but finding an effective manager will mean a great deal to you. The manager must measure up to the caliber of tenants you hope to attract. Only a manager with a good personal appearance, a pleasant manner, and the ability and willingness to work will be an asset. If you start having a vacancy problem and you are sure your rents are in line with those of your competitors, then most likely there is something wrong with the manager's performance.

The following is a check list of some of the rules to follow in instituting good management practices:

1. Screen prospective tenants carefully. Set up certain guidelines for minimum requirements below which you will not go, except in exceptional cases when tenants appear to be beyond reproach in all other respects. The point is to try to cull out unstable and undesirable tenants who are likely to stay only a short time or whose bad habits or inconsiderate attitudes would cause dissension among other tenants. The following hints might be helpful in this endeavour:

    A. Require that the tenant be employed continuously (and usually on the same job) for the past six months. This requirement can be bent sometimes for preferred students, or exceptional cases such as for retired persons and others who give an above-average appearance that they would be acceptable tenants and financially stable—not giving credence to the person who says "I'm financially independent," or "I get an allowance from my parents," or wherever from. One of the objectives of the stable job requirement is that you have a way to collect the rent in the event the tenant doesn't pay, and usually this insurance precludes your having to take any such action.

B. Check into prospective tenants' past rental histories. Have they been moving around a lot? And be wary when they give as a reference that they have been staying with friends, especially if the time span is substantial. Also, when a tenant wants to take the apartment "any time" or "right away," ask him how he can just up and move without giving notice to his present landlord. Their reasons may be legitimate, but you should check them out and don't believe everything they tell you. Their willingness to move in immediately, in the middle of the month, may be a sign that they are skipping out without giving notice to their present landlord, or that he has asked them to move—the latter may be difficult to verify, since some landlords will give an unwanted tenant a good reference just to get rid of him.

C. Watch for the hippy type. I am not speaking of people whose clothes are a little far out, but of the real hippy. The hippy will often clean himself up and may be able to make a reasonable presentation, at first glance. But if you look closely and watch their mannerisms and listen for little telltale clues, you can usually spot them. They usually send the girl friend out to look at the apartment, since it is a little easier for her to transform herself into a "straight" appearance.

Another telltale sign is when the tenant's work reference is from some boutique, self-employment, or some such thing. Also, watch out for landlord references which consist of "staying with friends," especially if the area where the friends live is not a very good one. Another real give-away is when the tenant is ready to pay cash on the spot (many do not have bank accounts—it is too "establishment"), and even offer to pay a couple of months' rent in advance. Never accept more than one month's rent from a tenant unless you are sure you want that tenant for a long time. Once a precedent has been set for payment of two or more months' rent in advance, you must then give an additional like amount of notice in order to evict the tenant.

Of course, not every hippy makes a bad tenant and they usually do pay their rent; but, by and large, hippies are undesirable tenants for many reasons, not the least of which is that you may rent to one or two persons and then find that the apartment is actually inhabited by half-a-dozen people, plus the invariable hoards of friends who visit constantly, sometimes to the point where the comings and goings resemble Grand Central Station on a holiday. And the crowning blow is that hippies usually play their stereo (or worse yet, musical instruments) so loud that it would drive any reasonably-oriented tenant out of the building.

2. Be sure to get a substantial security deposit to cover damages or infractions of the rental agreement, with the clear understanding that the deposit is refundable when the tenant moves, providing he has lived up to all the terms of the rental agreement.

Many owners collect a relatively small security deposit which is not refundable. It is a self-defeating practice. If the tenant knows he is not going to get his deposit refunded, then what is the incentive to take care of the apartment or to leave it in any reasonable condition? If the deposit is not refundable, the average tenant will leave an unkempt apartment, which may cause difficulty in getting a new tenant in right away, since cleaning must be arranged. Effective operation of income property depends upon the ability to have a new tenant move in immediately after an apartment has been vacated, thus avoiding loss of rent. Also, a tenant who does not have a refundable deposit at stake will usually be harder on the whole apartment and that will necessitate more frequent painting and higher maintenance costs.

If, on the other hand, the tenant knows he will get his deposit refunded if he leaves the premises presentable, then there will usually be no problem in renting the well-cared-for apartment and no delayed occupancy. Any minor cleaning that might be necessary can be taken care of without incident. So you can see the merits of having a smooth transition.

3. Don't gouge your tenants on the rent. A satisfied tenant who is not making demands for improvement deserves a lower rent than one who demands that everything be in perfect and immaculate condition. As your real estate holdings start to add up, you will appreciate more and more the merits of not disturbing good, long-term tenants. But, on the other hand, it is not necessary to give the rental away. A rough method I have found to be beneficial is to raise the rent on desirable existing tenants to a maximum of 90% of what the top rent should be. If the tenant then vacates, raise the rent about an additional five percent for the new tenant, thus still holding the rent a little below the market value. Some owners are more lenient and leave rentals at such a low level that it seems foolish.

There is a point beyond which a low rent is of no benefit to the owner. And, as I have often asked people who follow the practice of maintaining unusually low rents on their apartments (sometimes just because they like the tenant, even though no financial difficulty exists): "Would you take $40 or $50 (or whatever amount the apartment is under-rented) out of your pocket every month and hand it over to your tenant?" The answer is always the same, "of course not." But the way I see it, the principle is the same. If the owner can afford it, or if a particular tenant can't afford more rent, then it's a different matter. But do you know of any other market where the proprietor consistently takes a loss on his product because he "hates to charge" the going rate, or more if he can get it?

I had an interesting experience, a few years back, after I had purchased an apartment building and had raised the rents in order to cover the expenses and loan service, which was far greater than that of the previous owners who had owned the building for many years. The tenants had a couple of meetings and were considering a rent strike. They invited me to their last meeting and I went along to see what their objections were based on.

Quite a number of the tenants were complaining that they could not afford the rent increase. I told them that I was not a public assistance agency and that I could see no reason why I should undertake the job of subsidizing their rents, which is what I figured they were asking me to do. I said that if the other tenants were genuinely concerned about the plight of the ones claiming poverty, then perhaps they should be willing to contribute to their assistance, rather than ask me to carry the whole load. A couple of staunch supporters agreed to split the subsidy of one tenant with me. Then I told the ones who were crying poor mouth that if I were to give assistance, I would first require that they prove to me that they could not afford the increased rent, the same as they would be asked to do if they applied for public assistance.

It turned out that one of the tenants was eligible for Social Security benefits, which she had not applied for, since she did not like the idea of accepting Social Security benefits. I was dismayed and I asked her how she had the nerve to ask me for assistance when she was not even willing to collect Social Security benefits which she had paid for and which were certainly not to be looked down upon.

I also asked the tenants if they thought it fair to ask a total stranger—me—for assistance before they approached their immediate families on the subject.

What happened was, that the two staunch supporters, who had agreed to contribute to another tenant's assistance, moved out of the building about a week after the meeting, without giving notice. Only two of the tenants actually had a hardship, which I accepted without actual proof because I could sense their sincerity. I helped one to qualify for government rent subsidy, which she did not know was available, with the effect that she paid less out of pocket than she was paying before the rental increase. The other tenant's rent was left below all others in the building, and she is still there and her rent is still less than the others.'

I didn't hear any more about the rent strike. So if you are beset with a threatened rent strike, you may be able to embarrass the tenants into reasonable demands, if they have any sense of fair play at all. Ask them if the merchants reduce the price of their merchandise because their customers can't afford it.

4. Do not give out a lease if you are planning to sell the property, if it is a house or a building consisting of from two to four dwelling units. An exception to this might be when two or more of the units command fairly high rent, in which

PROPERTY MANAGEMENT

case it could be advantageous to have all but the most desirable of the high rent units leased. When more than one high rent unit is involved, a lease on all but one could serve to ease the mind of a prospective purchaser, as to potential vacancy problems. Very often, the unit you lease will be just the one the prospective purchaser would want to live in.

This holds true of larger income property also, if there is a particular unit which is exceptionally desirable or substantially larger than the other units. The owner will very often want to live on the top floor, unless there is something unusual about one of the lower floors which would cause the new owner to take a fancy to it.

5. Insist that all tenants sign a well-executed and binding rental agreement. Forms can usually be obtained from your local Real Estate Board for a nominal fee, or from most large stationery and office supply stores. Make sure that the form is filled out in duplicate, dated and signed, and that you give the tenant a copy. Be sure that the rental agreement states the terms on which the security deposit is held, and that a 30-day notice of intent to move is required; unless you are renting on a weekly or bi-weekly basis, in which case you would require a like amount of notice. Try to arrange for the rentals to come due on the first of each month. There is a multiple purpose behind this requirement. The first is that it saves you a lot of time in collecting all rents at the same time of the month. The second is that most desirable tenants are on this schedule and it is easier to rent an apartment, without rent loss, when it will be available on the first of the month.

6. Always insist on a written notice when a tenant gives notice of intent to vacate. When you receive the notice, start showing the apartment for rent as soon as practical. Many of the best tenants are organized and concerned to get an apartment lined up as soon they have decided to move. So

your early efforts will be rewarded with better tenants. However, since tenants shop more in the first couple of weeks of the month, the Johnny-on-the-spot approach to renting may result in more work.

As a rule, in the first couple of weeks of each month, tenants tend to be more choosy, often looking for something that is not available in their price range. So, if you want to cut down on the number of showings, wait until the middle of the month to make the big push to get it rented. By that time, the ones who are still looking will be a little more realistic about what they can afford and will also start to get a little concerned about getting a place before it is too late.

If the tenant only gives you 15 days notice, instead of the required 30 days, there should be no reason for concern. Just inform him that you will do your best to rent the apartment and that his notice to vacate will not affect the refund of his security deposit if you are able to rent the apartment by the time he vacates. This should insure good cooperation from the tenant when you want to show the apartment, and he is more likely to keep the apartment in presentable condition during the showing period. Anyway, in most areas it is illegal to collect rent from two parties for the same period on the same rental unit, except to cover damages, etc.

7. Keep on good terms with your tenants when possible. But don't hesitate to be firm with them when they get out of line—the sooner they find out who is running the show, the better. If you show any sign of weakness or reluctance to enforce the rules, some tenants will take it as a sign that they can do pretty much as they please. So be nice but firm, right from the start.

8. Keep the property in reasonable repair at all times. A leaking faucet or running toilet can run up the utility bill more than it would cost to make the necessary repairs, which

would eventually need fixing anyway—plus the fact that it makes for a happier tenant. And by all means keep the building and surrounding areas as neat and clean as practicable.

A word of caution against being overly fastidious. If you try to keep every building in perfect order, as you might your home, the costs may be prohibitive, unless you are operating luxury rentals.

9. One of the most distressing problems facing today's owners of residential rental property is the changing attitude of the tenants and the legislation giving tenants virtually unlimited rights, while the landlord is forced to take a back seat. But this need not be as bad as it might seem, and that is where the importance of doing a good job in screening your tenants comes in. You can weed out a lot of trouble-makers. Don't be so choosy, however, that you find everyone unacceptable and wind up with a lot of vacant apartments. It is sometimes better, if necessary, to take a chance on the tenant, rather than have a vacant apartment for an extended period of time.

At this writing I am happy to say that I have not been involved in a court battle with a tenant, for any cause. Most of the problems I have had with tenants came from those who were already in the buildings when I acquired them. Some of those buildings were for sale only because the tenants were refusing to move or to pay rent, which is not an insurmountable problem. And some good buys can be gotten in this way—a distressed seller is an anxious one. Usually, after acquiring a building with a problem tenant, I would have a talk with the tenant to see what the cause was. In many cases, it was simply a matter of complying with some simple demands the tenant had made.

On the other hand, if the tenant was truly lacking in cooperative spirit, a little persuasive talk would sometimes do the trick—like telling him that you would forget about the back rent and penalties he owed, if he would vacate by a certain date, giving a few days which would make it possible for him to find another apartment and comply.

Reminded often enough of the rent they owe and how their costs are going to mount if you are forced to hire an attorney to take legal action, tenants will usually move on their own. If further action is needed, then have an attorney send the tenant an eviction notice as soon as possible. After that, it is usually best not to undertake further discussions with the tenant. The implied authority behind an attorney's notice will often achieve the desired effect. In any case, have the attorney proceed with the eviction proceedings as rapidly as possible, until the required results have been obtained.

If you are forced to go through the whole legal process of evicting a tenant, it will be fairly costly. But waiting around, hoping the tenant will move is usually a losing battle and, after you have waited and lost more rent, you will have the same process to go through. However, you will find that very few tenants are willing to wait long enough for the sheriff to come to their door and take possession of their belongings and forcefully evict them. Probably, the most you would incur in the way of attorney fees would be for a letter and a summons. If you don't have the money, borrow it. The longer you wait, with a tenant not paying the rent, the less money you will have.

A trick I have seen used is to call the tenant and ask, "Has the sheriff got there yet?" This can be done whether or not there is any intention of getting the sheriff involved. It will have a remarkable effect on all but the most hardened offender, and it could, no doubt, cause some sleepless nights.

11

The Importance of Income Tax Guidance

Proper handling of your real estate ventures to insure maximum income tax advantage should be an important part of your overall efforts. Using the correct timing and tax planning can result in large tax savings. In addition, proper planning will sometimes defer the entire tax liability on the sale or exchange of a property, thus leaving you with more capital with which to invest.

IMPRACTICAL SELLING

In fact, the tax consequences of the sale of real estate are sometimes such that it becomes impractical to sell the property at all. That might sound a bit far-fetched, but it does apply in a situation where a sale would not net you enough cash to justify the loss of the property, and possibly not even enough cash with which to pay the capital gains tax the sale would require.

For example, let's assume you own a property with a market value of $70,000, for which you paid $40,000 three years before, that you made capital improvements in the amount of $5,000, and that you have written off depreciation on the property in the amount of $6,000. Essentially, your tax base would be figured by adding capital improvements to the purchase price, then deducting the depreciation, with a resultant tax base of $39,000. Your gain on the sale of the property would be $31,000.00, or approximately $26,000.00 after deducting the broker's fee and other selling expenses. Your maximum income tax liability from the sale would be $6,500; that is, a maximum of 25% of the net capital gain. Of course, the tax liability could be less, depending on your other income and deductions.

Now, suppose further, that you had refinanced the property after remodeling it and had received a loan of $56,000. (not taxable until the sale of the property, since funds received from refinancing real estate are not taxable). In this case, the maximum cash you would realize from the sale of the property would be approximately $14,000, an estimated $5,000 of which would go to pay selling expenses, including brokerage fee. Then, the approximate net cash in hand before taking into consideration any income tax liability would be $9,000. However, after income taxes (approximately 25% of the $26,000.00 net gain) that figure would be whittled down to about $2,500.00. The cash on hand would be further reduced if you were required to carry back secondary financing on the sale of the property. So you can see that for the amount of cash to be realized, the wisdom of selling a $70,000 property should be questioned—unless there was another compelling reason for the sale.

You could, however, consider a tax-free exchange of the property. The term "tax free" in reference to real property exchanges means only that you are deferring payment of taxes until some future date (tax is paid on the gain when you eventually sell the property for which you traded), but it has the advantage of giving you the interest-free use of the money in the interim.

SALE OF PERSONAL RESIDENCE

Another way to defer capital gains tax is on the sale of your personal residence. In order to qualify, however, you must meet certain requirements which are roughly as follows:

1. You must buy and use your new residence within one year before or after you sell your old one.

2. You must have used your old residence as your principal place of residence and you must use your new residence as your principal place of residence.

3. The cost of the new residence must at least equal the adjusted sales price (sales price, less selling expenses) of the old one. In the event your new residence costs less than your old one, tax must be paid on the difference in the two prices. However, you need not invest all, or any set portion, of the proceeds from the sale of your old residence, when purchasing your new one. You may purchase the new residence with a low down payment and do what you like with the balance of the funds. Also, the term "residence" does not exclude a two-or-more-unit dwelling. However, only the percentage portion of the total property that you used as your residence may be considered. For example, if you owned a three-unit building and occupied one-third of the building, only one-third of the sales price may be transferred to your new residence. You must pay capital gains tax on the remainder.

If you defer tax on your residence, you will need to keep a record of all expenses incurred in fixing up either or both properties until such time as you sell and declare the capital gain, even though the time span may cover a period of many years Failure to keep proper records and receipts could result in disallowance of the fix-up expenses. The miscellaneous costs of keeping up a residence, such as regular maintenance items, are not deductible and may not be added to the cost of the residence. However, any cost which can be considered an improvement may be added to the cost of the residence, thus reducing the gain on which you would be taxed. Before making any move where tax deferral may be an important consideration, be sure to consult a tax expert regarding all the requirements you must meet, just to be on the safe side.

LEARN ABOUT CAPITAL GAINS

There are many ways in which you can effect tax savings, so it would be well worth your while to spend some time learning the basics of the capital gains tax laws as applied to real estate, thus enabling you to take advantage of the opportunities and options open to you. Also, having a basic knowledge of the tax laws would be helpful in planning your overall investment approach.

Beware of relying on tax information obtained from calling your local IRS information service. Unfortunately, the people they have giving out information are often not qualified to handle complicated or complex tax questions. I have received a lot of mis-information from the IRS advisors. Fortunately, I usually knew enough to know that their information was incorrect, even though I did not know exactly what the correct answer was.

PLAN YOUR TAXES

A sampling of things to watch for in your tax planning, relating to the sale or transfer of real estate are:

1. If you sell a building that would qualify as your home, you may be able to transfer your tax liability to your new home, as described above. By the term "new home" it is not meant to indicate that the house must be new, it is simply a means of referring to your most recent acquisition.

2. Be sure to keep all your receipts for remodeling expenses, maintenance and repairs, and any other expenses related to the operation of real estate. Some of these expenses, however, may not be deductible on your home, depending on the time of the expenditure in relation to the time your home was sold. So, if you are contemplating considerable redecorating prior to the sale of your house, check out the requirements for the allowance of these expenses as deductions.

3. Unless you are prepared to forfeit the advantage of the capital gains tax treatment on your gain, be sure you have held the property for more than six months.

4. You may want to take advantage of the accelerated depreciation allowance, particularly if you plan to keep the property for a number of years, during which time you can recapture some of the accelerated depreciation so that you will not be required to pay a straight income tax rate on that portion of the ac-

celerated depreciation which is recaptured. I won't try to explain further here. It can get quite complicated. The fact that you know of its existence is sufficient for now. When you plan to take accelerated depreciation on your property, check out the tax law thoroughly so you can plan wisely.

5. You may be able to write off furniture, and some other appurtenances to the building, at an accelerated rate which would not be applicable to the building as a whole. In addition, check into the extra first-year allowance for depreciation on furniture.

6. You may be able to write off a portion of your automobile expenses, including depreciation, if your real estate investments require the use of your automobile, as they almost surely will.

7. Before selling a property, you may want to consider the consequences of the sale. If the property is one you would like to keep, but you want to get some cash out of it, you may want to refinance and hold the property for further appreciation and tax write-offs. But, also consider the high cost of refinancing.

8. The loan fees paid for securing financing or for paying off existing loans (prepayment penalties) may be deductible as interest, rather than added to the cost basis of the property, as had been the case until the fairly recent change in the tax law.

12

Financing

The real key to successful rapid advancement in real estate is in financing. The idea is to work with someone else's money to the extent possible without taxing your ability to comfortably service the loans. Leverage gives you flexibility. Without leverage, real estate investments, for the most part, would cease to be attractive ventures. For example, if you have $5,000 invested in real estate that you purchased for $50,000 and the increase in value at the end of the first year was $1,500, then you would have a 30% increase in your capital investment. The $1,500 increase in value is figured at the rate of three-percent per year, which is a conservative estimate by anyone's reckoning, and I expect appreciation to exceed that figure by a wide margin during the next few years. Of course, if you got a bargain when you purchased the property and then made improvements which would increase its value substantially, the percentage return of your investment would soar. On the other hand, if you had paid all cash for the same $50,000 property, your percentage increase would be nominal, using the same formula as outlined above.

DON'T BE AFRAID OF JUNIOR MORTGAGES

One of the most foolish things I have ever heard said is, "Don't buy a building with more than one loan on it." The person who gives or adheres to that advice would not be hesitant to purchase a building with a ten percent cash down payment and a 90% first loan. But the same person would turn down the same property with a 70% first loan and a 20% second loan; or perhaps even a 70% first loan and a 15% second and an additional five percent third loan—even though the total payments and combined interest payments might be the same. There are times when junior loans on a property may be undesirable, particularly if there is any question of your being able to increase the first loan to help wipe them out when you are ready to sell—since it is anticipated that you will have a higher price tag than when you purchased the property, necessitating either a larger down payment or more financing.

Sometimes the number of loans or the interest rate, either on the first or junior mortgages, are of relatively little importance to the investment as a whole, as long as there is no question that you will be able to meet the monthly obligations. But do take the necessary precautions to make sure that you will not get "locked in" with several loans on a property and no prospect of resolving them. Although multiple junior loans should not deter you as a purchaser of a property, under favorable conditions, you need to recognize that a couple of junior loans on a rehabilitated property which is being offered at a top price could be a serious handicap, unless the buyer could obtain a new increased first loan to assist with the purchase.

As a rule, properties in poor showing condition have the best prospects for making a large profit. But as a result of their condition, it is usually difficult to obtain favorable financing terms on such properties. The first loan you can anticipate from conventional sources would be for a lesser percentage of the sales price and at a higher rate of interest than would be available on property in first rate condition. The result is that secondary financing is the rule, rather than the exception. But when you have the property showing in good condition, it should be possible to get an increased loan.

DON'T BE AFRAID TO BORROW MONEY

Don't worry about how much you owe on real estate, as long as you are confident that you will have the means to meet your obligations, with a reasonable amount of funds in reserve. If the loans you owe on the property are purchase money mortgages (a mortgage that is executed by the purchaser as part of the purchase price), then the sole security for a mortgage is the property which secures it. So, all you can lose is what you have invested in the property, and a blemish on your credit rating. However, if you follow reasonably sound investment practices, there should be no reason to worry about meeting your obligations.

So don't be a worry wart. But if you are, it may console you to know that I have seen investors get so emotional and nervous when they sign for their first real estate venture, that they are practically basket cases for days. In fact, I have a good friend (I hope his sense of humor is in order) who was a nervous wreck for days after purchasing one half (with a partner) of a $16,000 pair of flats—just about the least expensive building available at the time. He admitted that financial obligations of any kind had always bothered him. However, he has since purchased several properties and upgraded himself into a very nice home with no signs of concern about the mortgage debt. So, if your first purchase leaves you a bit upset for a while, don't worry. You'll get over it. But if it bothers you too much, it may be a sign that the world of high finance is not your bag.

PRIME SOURCES OF FINANCING

It may be that you can take advantage of the FHA or VA loans, if you are purchasing a relatively new building. These sources of financing can be helpful as a means of purchasing with little or no down payment. But, as a rule, the FHA and VA loans are unavailable when purchasing older buildings in need of repair. In fact, FHA and VA appraisals on old buildings often fail to come anywhere near the actual market value—even more so when the property is in an area that might be considered less than prime. It's ironic that a source of financing backed by our federal government has consistently practiced discrimination but it's a fact, though they use other excuses for not lending in certain areas, or not giving a loan commitment that anyone could use. The situation has improved some in recent years, but discriminatory practices still exist.

Another problem is that FHA and VA appraisers require that the properties be put in mint condition before the loan is put on, so how can you use them on any property that needs work? And even when available, FHA and VA loans are not necessarily any better than conventional financing. The high loan fees and origination fees and mandatory loan insurance, etc. that are required often make the overall cost of the loans as high or higher than conventional loans. So, if you have an alternative method of financing, it might be worth while to compare the merits of each source after determining the total overall costs of each.

If you have a good relationship with your bank, you may be able to get reasonable financing there, but you will find that most banks are extremely conservative when lending on properties that are not in good condition, and that insurance company lenders are even more conservative. Both sources are reluctant to lend when secondary financing is involved.

But lending policies vary so much from one institution to another, and from one locale to another, that it may be worth checking out before you discount the source. If the financing is available at your bank, it may be that you can obtain better terms than would be available at the savings and loan associations—particularly on the prepayment penalty, which could be a large savings in the event you are required to pay off the loan when the property is sold, rather than transfer it to the new owner. But bank loans are seldom automatically transferrable to a new owner, which can be somewhat restrictive and financially costly if there is a prepayment penalty clause in your bank mortgage agreement. On the other hand, savings and loan associations will usually transfer the loan if the buyer can meet their credit requirements.

Banks are a good source of home improvement loans, although they usually require that the borrower have a certain percentage of equity in the property (about 20% of their appraisal value), so don't assume that you can automatically obtain a home improvement loan.

Banks and insurance companies are prime sources of financing for large, primarily new projects. But when it comes to financing existing structures that are in need of considerable repair or decorating, they will most likely prove to be very reluctant lenders. But, again, check out all the sources until you have a fairly good idea what to expect.

Your broker should be able to fill you in with a fair degree of accuracy.

As a rule you will find that what it boils down to is that the main sources of financing available for your projects will be either private (usually the seller) or the savings and loan associations. In addition to normal first loans, an additional source of financing from the savings and loan associations is what is referred to in the business as the "hold back loan." The hold back loan can be useful when you plan to do substantial remodeling. The association, after appraising the property, will give you a commitment that they will lend a certain amount based on the existing condition of the property, with an additional specified amount to be released upon completion of certain specified improvements. So the loan commitment is actually for the total of the basic commitment plus the amount of the hold back. When the property is in need of considerable repair, some primary loans are given only with the requirement that the buyer make certain improvements. At other times, the buyer will need to request the hold-back loan. The advantage of this type of financing is that it is not necessary for the investor to tie up large sums of money in order to perform the necessary remodeling, with the added advantage that when the work is completed and the additional advance released, the larger amount of the loan may be helpful in reselling the property. In essence, what the hold-back loan does is to recover your improvement costs without the necessity of costly refinancing or selling proceedings.

WHAT ABOUT BALLOON PAYMENTS?

A balloon payment is a lump sum that becomes due at the end of a mortgage term as a result of a loan with pay-

FINANCING   121

ments which were not fully amortized over the life of the loan. Most junior loans are payable at the rate of one percent per month of the original balance (or more at buyer's option), including principal and interest. Thus, a $5,000 loan payable $50 per month at nine percent interest would take approximately 15 years to amortize in full. However, a junior loan of $5,000 would usually be due in full in approximately five years, which would leave a substantial balloon payment due, if amortization is figured on the basis of one percent per month. The maturity date and the interest rate and other terms of secondary financing are negotiable points. Normally, the larger the loan, the longer the term of the note, but there is no set rule and the terms are strictly a matter of negotiation between the buyer and seller or other lender, as the case may be.

At the time of acquiring a property where you are going to have a second loan, if you think you may need to transfer the second loan when you eventually sell, you should try to negotiate the loan so that it will not be due on sale of the property, and for as long a term as possible.

Be cautious about accepting short-term mortgages with extremely large balloon payments. Be reasonably sure that you will have some means of taking care of the balloon payment in the event you hold the property until the loan matures. This can be accomplished by refinancing, selling, or floating a new second loan. There is usually a remedy for paying off reasonable balloon payments, so don't lose out on all the good opportunities by being overly-concerned about them.

13

Remodeling

The difference between losing money, breaking even, and making substantial profit on a real estate investment often depends on your approach to remodeling or decorating the property. You will need to remember, at all times, that your goal is to improve the property in a practical manner, as inexpensively as possible, in order to get the desired results—to keep your costs down by sticking to changes that are either essential or that will noticeably improve the property.

Essentially, you should gear your remodeling and decorating to suit the needs and tastes of the class and type of customers who are most likely to purchase your property. The majority of the likely residents of most areas can be categorized—such as unmarried persons; young childless couples; small families; large families; elderly couples; low, middle or high income, etc. Of course, the size of the house or units and the number of bedrooms and bathrooms will dictate the family makeup to which you will need to cater, but you should be aware of that makeup so you can prepare the property accordingly. Put on your thinking cap and list the amenities of your investment and then see whose needs would best be satisfied by the particular property. Also, consider whether certain changes would be worth while in order to make the property desirable to a wider range of prospects. Many times, improvements are made simply at the whim of the owner without considering whether the changes are practical or whether they would likely appeal to the prospective tenants or purchasers. The result is, ultimately, much higher costs and less profit.

MAKING THE RIGHT IMPROVEMENTS

Will the change you are contemplating actually increase the value of the property? A good rule of thumb would be that for every dollar spent in remodeling or decorating, you should increase the value of the property by at least three dollars. It is not always possible to apply this rule, and I am not suggesting that you adopt a strict adherence to it, but it will be helpful in giving you perspective at times when you are not sure which course to take.

If you acquire an old building with high ceilings, unless you can effectively change the character of the entire building, inside and out, to that of a modern structure, do not even think of lowering the ceilings. Whether you personally like the high ceilings and ornate trimming is not the point, unless you plan to live in the building for a long time. Many people do like the high ceilings, and particularly those who are interested in the charm of older buildings. In addition to the considerable cost and effort of lowering the ceilings, and other such character changes, such a move would almost surely lower the value of the building considerably. If you have any doubts at all, leave the high ceilings and extra trim intact. I have seen buildings where well-meaning owners removed all the trim, lowered the ceilings, etc., with the result of reducing the market value of the building, in addition to the loss of all the costs of the work performed.

Modern kitchens and baths are usually appreciated in any type of building. However, decorating around the existing fixtures is sometimes preferable to the costly project of installing all new ones. A little imagination and innovative decorating can do wonders and it sometimes produces a more salable product than would all new fixtures of poor or obviously inexpensive quality.

Whatever work you decide to do, above all be sure to insist on quality workmanship. There is nothing harder to sell than shoddy workmanship of any kind. I have seen many properties become dogs on the market due to the effects of poor workmanship. Just ask yourself: would you want to pay the higher price of a remodeled house if you had the feeling that the work would need to be re-done in order to be acceptable?

Before you purchase a property with the express purpose of converting the building into more dwelling units than are existing, be sure that the local building codes and zoning ordinances will allow such a change. There are many restrictions placed on increasing the number of dwelling units, such as requiring additional parking, additional fireproofing of the building, additional means of egress, and many others. The requirements vary greatly from one city or county to another, so check the local building code through the building inspection department before committing yourself to purchase.

One of the most important things to watch, and often the most difficult to control, is that you do not over-spend, or over-improve the property. Always watch your expenditures, and even more so when the area does not warrant an elaborate and expensively decorated property.

DON'T GET STUNG BY BUILDING CONTRACTORS

By building contractors, I am referring to anyone whose services you might require in the process of remodeling a building, whether it be an electrician, plumber, general contractor, or just a "handy man." But my comments are aimed primarily at the general contractor and the "handy man."

Always hire a worker or contractor whose work you know will be good, as opposed to a less expensive alternative who may not be a professional and the quality of whose work you do not know. If in doubt, give the contractor a small job to see how well he performs. Almost all contractors will assure you that they have unlimited experience and that they can, and will, perform all tasks in a professional manner. But the truth is that most unlicensed workmen do deplorable work, as do a smaller percentage of the professionals.

Be extremely wary of the high-pressure contractor, often unlicensed, who offers to do the job at some low figure. What you pay for is what you get, as a rule. And there is no doubt about it, a job well done is almost invaluable as opposed to a slovenly job. I do not know of anything that will turn a buyer off faster than poor workmanship.

And, by all means, try to avoid the sharpie contractor's tactics of getting as much advance payment as possible, and then disappearing on another job for weeks, or even months, leaving you with an unfinished job and a written commitment to have that particular contractor perform the work. Most small contractors have several jobs going at the same time. As a result, most of their work is concentrated with the person who has tied them down to a written contract including a deadline and penalty clause for work not performed on time.

Don't make advance payments to the contractor for more than what will cover about 75% of the amount of work actually completed, except when it is necessary to give an initial advance for materials. One of the favorite tricks of the sharp operator is to breeze through the portion of the job that will progress rapidly, giving the appearance that the job is almost completed, at the same time pressuring for additional advances. Then, when he has received most of the money for the job, he becomes unavailable, with a seemingly small amount of work remaining to be completed that may actually be the larger portion of the total job.

And never make the final payment to a contractor until you have thoroughly checked out the work and are satisfied that everything is in order. For example, a painting contractor may have done a beautiful job overall; but, when the paint dried, did he unstick the windows so they will open and close? Once a contractor is paid in full and has left the job, it is very difficult and sometimes impossible to get him back for small corrective work.

Actually, you should not have any real difficulty if you use basic common sense in protecting yourself and do not allow yourself to become dissuaded from taking the necessary precautions to see that you will get all that you are paying for, the quality you are paying for, and that it will be performed when you want it. I don't want to discredit all contractors, but remodeling contractors in particular seem to be a strange breed as a whole. Even with the best of intentions, it seems that they are prone to get caught in a time squeeze by over-committing themselves. It appears to be an occupational hazard.

DECORATING

Before making any improvement, consider first the approximate cost, then consider whether that particular improvement would proportionately enhance the value of the property. If the project is simply a matter of decorating, with no substantial change in the fixtures or the structure itself, the cost may not be as important as whether the change will actually be an improvement at all. I cannot stress too strongly the importance of making sure that what you are considering to be an improvement will be seen the same way in the eyes of others. For assistance in formulating some decorating ideas, you may find some of the home decorating magazines helpful.

I have found that the best course to take in decorating is to be reasonably conservative. Decorating is a very personal thing. By far the most practical and widely-accepted approach to painting, for example, is to paint almost everything off-white. Don't use stark white because it is too harsh and it does not cover very well, thus requiring more coats of paint. Off-white may not be everyone's ideal, but it will come closer than most attempts at using various colors. Sticking with one color also has the tremendous advantage of not having a lot of costly leftovers which would need labeling, storing, etc., in case you need to do some touching up at a later date. You can realize substantial savings by purchasing in quantity, if you use one uniform color everywhere. Off-white will complement any color furniture and decorating accessories. If you feel a strong urge to use some colors and feel that your judgment is up to the task of trying to please the masses, then first try your luck in the kitchen and bath rooms.

The type of flooring you should use depends a great deal on the type of building you are decorating. If it is Victorian, or some similar old-style building, then hardwood floors are very often preferred by the prospective buyers and tenants. In any case, if there are existing hardwood floors, I would never advise covering them with carpeting. If the building is modern, then wall-to-wall carpeting would usually be in order and more widely appreciated.

In selecting carpet colors, stick to the rule of being conservative. Your favorite color may not appeal to others, or it may clash with their furnishings. The color I have found to receive wide acceptance is gold. A medium gold is best, since light gold shows dirt too easily. Gold will go with just about anything, and will complement most other colors. In any case, remember to be conservative, unless you are an accomplished decorator, in which case you may do well with considerably more leeway. For everyone, and especially for the professional decorator, my main caution would be not to over-spend. It is easy to get carried away and invest more than is practical for the particular investment.

14

How to Negotiate

TO BUY

Your success in buying the right property at the right time, at the right price, and on the right terms will depend a great deal on your capacity for skillful negotiating. The following check list should give you enough guidance so that you can compete with the best of them.

1. Price and terms to offer

Don't be swayed too much by the broker's comments on what price he thinks the seller will accept, or whether the seller will carry back either first or secondary financing. Listen attentively, because he may give you some helpful clues; but, in the end, make up your own mind and offer as little as you think would be to your benefit. The problem is—assuming the broker has your interest at heart in the first place—that many brokers do not have the foggiest notion of what a seller will accept, though most are not short on opinions about the subject.

Sellers usually do not know what they will accept until they are confronted with a bona fide offer and it has been hashed over thoroughly and sometimes slept on. So, don't be influenced too much by anything either a broker or seller might say regarding the price or the terms the seller will accept. I have often heard the broker and seller both say that the price was FIRM, but when an offer came in at a considerably lower price, the seller re-considered and accepted, or at least gave a reasonable counteroffer. And if you make a very low offer, don't be surprised if the seller refuses to counteroffer, or comes back with a counteroffer substantially the same as the asking price. If you are seriously interested, try it again at a little higher price and you may get a more favorable response.

The same situation prevails with the seller carrying back a first or second loan. Make your offer, and you'll have a better idea when you get the seller's response. Very often, the seller can be persuaded to change his mind if your broker presents objective and reasonable arguments. I have known cases where the seller had been insisting on an all cash sale, when it was actually to his benefit to carry back some financing, which was arranged after this point was brought out.

The real key is to find out why a person is selling. Does he need, or is he going to invest, all the cash proceeds from the sale? If not, the interest you can offer him on a note secured by a deed of trust on the property may be substantially more than he would get from other sources. A good broker can be of invaluable assistance along these lines, just as a not so good broker will lose the deal for you.

If you are up against a stubborn seller who has a price in his head and won't change it, it may be very effective to ask the seller how he arrived at that particular price. Or if you are dealing with a broker, as is usually the case, ask the broker to find out from the seller how he arrived at the price. It will have a very sobering effect on some sellers. Very often, they do not have a formula and have arrived at the price arbitrarily. Under such conditions, be prepared to explain how you arrived at the price you are willing to pay, but only if you are asked. You can get by, in the absence of a persuasive appraisal method, by simply saying that you have a complicated method that has proved infallible, and give no further explanation.

2. Don't act anxious

Don't let the seller or broker know how anxious you are to get the property. Act as unconcerned as possible, beyond letting them know that you would like to purchase it. It sometimes helps to let it be known that you are considering other properties, though your disclosure of that fact should be discreet in order to have maximum effect. Rather than stating flatly that you are interested in another property, just make some statement that will make the seller, or broker, arrive at that conclusion.

3. Keep your deposit small

Always put up as little initial deposit as possible when making an offer, and never turn the deposit over to the owner. Give it to the broker or put it directly in escrow. In the event you get involved in a situation where it becomes advantageous for you to back out of the deal later on, you may be forced to forfeit the deposit. If you back out without a legitimate excuse, theoretically the seller can seek court action for specific performance of the contract, though this is seldom done since the outcome is always questionable and the costs are so high—plus the disadvantage of tying up the property for a long period while you are waiting for a court decision.

4. Regarding private financing

When you are asking the seller to carry back either the first mortgage or a junior mortgage, be sure to:

A. ALWAYS put in the "or more" clause; that is, you state that your payments are so many dollars, "or more," per month. . . . In the absence of the "or more" clause, the holder of the note could refuse to accept payment when you have sold the property and want to pay off the loan. The holder of a note without a "due on sale" clause could thus actually prevent or hold up the sale of the property, unless the note has an "or more" clause. The holder of such a note could claim that he is not obligated to accept anything over and above the specified payments.

B. ALWAYS state the dollar amount of your payments or a clause such as "one percent per month, or more."

C. ALWAYS state the rate of interest you expect to pay, along with your demand as to what you want in the way of points, loan fee, and maximum pre-payment penalty. The prepayment penalty is usually approximately two percent of the balance owing at the time of the payoff; however prepayment penalties vary greatly with different lenders. The reason for specifying the exact terms you want on your original agreement to purchase is so that you will have the option to refuse any loan commitment that is not acceptable. It would be a good idea to find out what the average loan fees and prepayment penalties are in your area so you can be realistic about your demands. It is safe to say that many brokers will not know lenders' policies regarding prepayment penalties, so you may need to call the lenders and inquire directly.

The only reason I am stressing the prepayment penalties is that in recent years, when funds were in short supply and interest rates were high, some lending institutions changed their prepayment penalty from the previous average of about two percent to as much as five or six percent of the amount of the loan. And just because funds may have become more available does not necessarily mean that the lender has changed the prepayment penalty back to a more reasonable figure.

D. ALWAYS insist on either a final due date (such as "five years from date of execution"), or the statement "until paid in full." Try to get the offer through without a clause stating that the note is due on sale, since the less obvious you make the point, the better chance you will stand of getting it approved by the seller. If the "due on sale" clause is not included on your ratified offer, and subsequently the note, then the note is automatically transferrable to any future purchaser, which would sometimes be helpful in selling the property without the necessity of your carrying secondary financing. This may be variable under different state laws.

E. ALWAYS try to insert some contingency clause which is not obvious, such as subject to some unobtainable financing, or subject to further inspection and approval of the property, but which would give you a way out of the deal in case you decide some time before closing that you do not want to purchase the property. If all the conditions of the ratified offer have been met, or if you have otherwise removed all the contingencies, then you are obligated to go through with the deal.

There are ways out of such a situation, but in the absence of a contingency that has not been met, you would almost surely lose your initial deposit. Also, the contingency clause can sometimes be used to get the seller to lower the price, by threatening to pull out of the deal because one thing or another does not come up to your original expectations, though you should be prepared to lose the deal if you attempt this—the seller might be angered to the point where he would refuse to go through with the deal.

F. In your offer, ALWAYS stipulate that there are to be no violations or complaints on record with any public works department (unless such violations or complaints have been made known to you and are already covered in the offer). Even though the seller is obligated by law to divulge to the buyer any work required, many sellers will avoid the issue unless confronted directly. Indeed some will lie about it, no matter how they are approached. But if it is in writing, you will have recourse. Also, state laws vary.

5. Watch out for possible leases

Specify in your offer that no part of the property is to be on lease, except the specified portion that has been represented to you as being leased. In the case of existing leases, make your offer subject to your inspection and approval of the leases.

6. Know what is included in the price

Be sure to spell out in the offer exactly what you expect to get with the property in the way of fixtures not obviously affixed to the property. And if affixed, it could still be necessary to list the items individually when they are of considerable value, such as wall-to-wall carpeting, an expensive chandelier, etc. You can use catch-all phrases like "including all furniture and fixtures presently used in the rental and operation of the property and not belonging to the tenants" for rental property. For homes, specify each item separately, if it is important to the purchase. If you have not been specific about what is to be included in the sale, some sellers will practically strip the property before they turn it over to you. Their actions may be illegal, but it may be too expensive to press the legal issue. Also the laws are not always explicit.

7. Title insurance is a must

Always insist on title insurance when you are purchasing real estate, and before closing the deal, be sure to read the title conditions as stated on the title insurance policy or the preliminary title search. Title insurance essentially insures that there are no liens, encumbrances, easements, encroachments, or other clouds on the title, other than the ones that are stated in the title insurance policy. It is surprising how few buyers, or even brokers, actually read the title insurance policy before taking title to the property. If you find an objectionable cloud on the title, that was not previously brought to your attention by the seller or the broker, then it may be a legitimate excuse to rescind the deal—if you so choose—unless the cloud can be removed from the title during the escrow period provided by the sales agreement or any extension of time provided therein. But don't be convinced by some smooth talker that you do not need title insurance and that you would save a lot of money by not bothering with title insurance. It's not worth the risk of getting a property with an unmarketable title.

Right after I first went into real estate I was almost talked into foregoing the title insurance on a house I was considering purchasing. As a matter of fact, the smooth talker would have succeeded if he hadn't been so persistent in his efforts to "save me money." I became suspicious that something was wrong and decided against the property altogether. A couple of years later, quite by accident, I discovered that I was right about my suspicions. The same property was again for sale, with different owners who had purchased it without title insurance. I showed the property to some prospects who made an offer and the sale was consummated. When the title search was made, it turned up that there was a discrepancy in one of the lot lines. It could have resulted in a costly legal battle or an unmarketable property, but fortunately the title company was eventually able to resolve the problem. Much worse things than that could happen if you do not get title insurance.

8. Take into consideration the seller's reason for selling

Don't get hung up on insisting that the seller move out some tenants before the close of escrow. It is all right to ask for this service if you feel it is important—though it would be best to wait until most of the other terms of sale are agreed upon before you put it in your demands. But to insist on it at all may be impractical, since the only reason the seller is willing to part with the property at the agreed price will sometimes be because he is having problems with the tenants. So, since what the seller may want most is to be relieved of the burden, it would be to your advantage to negotiate more on the price and other terms and take the responsibility of handling the tenants yourself—providing you have the funds to carry the property until the tenant problem can be resolved.

With all the above negotiating tips in mind, don't lose sight of your main objective. Basically, what you want is to purchase the property for as low a price and on terms that are as favorable as practicable. Sometimes, the less you ask for in your offer, and the simpler you can make the deal, the better price you are likely to get. If the seller is hung up on some issue, ask yourself if it is worth killing the deal or whether you could easily make it up by negotiating on more important points where the seller may be more flexible. For example, if a very attractive chandelier is important to the seller and he wants to take it with him, just forget about the chandelier and negotiate on the price or other terms. He may be so relieved that you are letting him keep the chandelier that he will be very agreeable on other points.

One other thing, don't haggle about interest when the price or other considerations are more important. If you are planning to keep the property for only a short while, a little more interest on the second or third note should be of relatively little importance to you. In fact, I have seen many instances where the seller was so pleased with the high interest rate he was getting on a small note, that he would make other important concessions. And I have seen buyers lose deals, or pay higher prices than could have been arranged, because they were unwilling to pay 10% interest on a $4,000 second loan with a three-year due date. The difference of one percent interest on that loan is only approximately $40 per year. Chances were that the buyer would not hold the property more than a year, so how important are the one or two percentage points on the interest rate? The possible exception to the above attitude is when the seller is carrying back a substantial first or second loan that you would expect to transfer to the new owner when you sold, in which case the terms of the loan could be important.

The best bargains I have gotten in real estate, without exception I think, have been available to me because, unlike most other prospective purchasers, I was willing to let the seller have his way on points that were creating an impasse. But, since I was able to switch my efforts to another facet of the negotiations, I realized other substantial gains. On one property I was purchasing, I even gave up a $15,000 commission because, in the middle of negotiations, the seller decided that he would not pay me a commission. I simply negotiated the price and terms to the point that, in the long run, I came out ahead of my original offer which included a $15,000 commission to me. That seller had a very difficult and unreasonable attorney representing him, and that was the basis of the problem. The attorney actually did an injustice to his client in the way he handled the deal. But the point is that it helps to be flexible, and particularly when you are able to replace what you are giving up with something just as good or better.

Another interesting case comes to mind. It concerns the unreasonable demands of a buyer whom I represented a few years back. This buyer made an offer to purchase a property, with a requirement that the seller carry back a $5,000 interest-free second note for a period of one year. The seller was so incensed by this unusual demand that he refused the deal, even though the total proceeds from the sale, exclusive of interest on the note, were more than adequate. In the end, I had to pay the seller $400 to cover reasonable interest on the note for the one-year period.

In this case, both the buyer and seller were acting foolishly. The buyer, I discovered later, was the type who would not purchase a property unless he was able to get something free. He could have gotten a better price on the property if he had negotiated on the price, rather than trying to save a little money on interest. The seller, on the other hand, could have gotten an even higher price if he had been willing to go along with the interest-free loan. So, it's not how you get it, but how much you get that counts.

Actually, before you make a final commitment on your first purchase or two, you should see a real estate attorney to make sure everything is in order. I say this with the hope that you will get a realistic attorney who will stick to the essentials and not complicate the negotiations by concentrating on all the wrong things or changing wording which is not important. But you may need protection, so it's better to be safe and over-protected than sorry. But get your money's worth and ask the attorney any questions you may have concerning the present or potential future deals and make notes so you will know what to do in the future, possibly without further consultation with an attorney.

TO SELL

In addition to the points given in this section to assist in your negotiations as a seller, it would also be to your benefit to keep in mind many of the points brought up for negotiating as a buyer. Because, as a seller, you need to be alert to some of the techniques that prospective purchasers may be applying. Whether you are the buyer or seller, it often helps to cope with the other party's tactics by putting yourself in his shoes and thinking in terms of what you would do in his place. You will see that small things sometimes go a long way toward helping to achieve your goal of obtaining the maximum selling price in a reasonable length of time. A responsible broker should be able to guide you through negotiations to keep you from making serious mistakes. However, since some brokers are not responsible and since there are many brokers who do not themselves know enough to be of much assistance in protecting you, the following points may be helpful:

1. Set your own price

Although it is sometimes necessary to seek the advice of brokers as to the potential value of your property, there are problems in trying to sort out the brokers' estimates of the value of your property. Some brokers will give you a low price in order to expedite the sale; some will give you a high price in order to beat out the competition and get the listing for their office, with the idea of getting a price reduction after the listing is tied up. Then there are other brokers who will give you their honest opinions of the value, but they may not be knowledgeable enough to be accurate. So, in the end, it is up to you to evaluate all the information you receive and then determine the final asking price.

But don't set your price unrealistically high with the hope that someone just might buy it at that price. Your property will become shopworn, with the result that when you finally get down to a reasonable price, it may be difficult to get anyone interested. The best asking price is one where you have allowed approximately ten percent leeway for negotiating. If the broker gives you a hard time because you paid substantially less than you are asking, then ask him, "If I had paid more for the property, would that have made it a better value? If I had paid a million dollars for it, would someone pay me a million, just because I paid it?" What this will hopefully get across is that what you paid for the property has no bearing on its value. I have seen many properties sell two or three times in the course of one year's time, each time at a substantially higher price, often with no changes having been made in the property.

2. Make the property available

It is important that your property be as easy to show as you can possibly arrange. Most properties that are difficult to show, for whatever reason, never get shown to most of the prospects who would be interested in seeing them. Brokers can and should screen the prospects so as to avoid obviously unnecessary showings, but it is often difficult to second-guess the buyer. So be patient if it seems as if there are too many lookers and not enough buyers. You never know which one will buy.

3. Watch for phony offers

Be alert to the fact that some brokers make a practice of submitting phony offers in order to get the price reduced, or the broker may encourage an uninterested client to submit a low offer on the chance that he might get a real bargain. The broker then uses the low offer to try to get the asking price reduced. It could be that a low offer your broker brings in is a bona fide offer. But even so—as you will see and probably will do sometimes yourself—some prospective buyers who are seriously interested in a property will make a low offer—a just-in-case offer. So don't discount low offers too quickly, since the prospect may be genuinely interested. It has always been my advice for the seller to at least make a counteroffer, even if the counteroffer is near the asking price. It is not a good idea, however, to counteroffer at your rock bottom price, unless your prospective buyer has made an offer reasonably near that figure.

4. Avoiding the contingency pitfalls

When you receive an offer on your property, you should attempt to cut the buyer's escape clauses (contingencies) to a minimum, to the extent possible without discouraging the buyer altogether. Watch for contingencies the buyer has inserted that could tie up your property (since it is usually taken off the market while a ratified deal is pending) for long periods of time, especially if time is an important factor, as it usually is. For example, if you have a 30-day closing period and the buyer has made an offer subject to obtaining a specified loan on specific terms, etc., it might be wise to limit the time in which you allow the buyer to obtain a firm loan commitment to a period of 15 days, or some reasonable period, depending on the prospects of getting the requested loan. This is very important when the prospects of obtaining the requested terms look questionable. If you know for certain they are unobtainable, it might be a good idea to change the figures to something more realistic. If, however, the buyer remains adamant about trying to get the terms, then it would usually be wise to go along with him in the hope that he will actually accept the best obtainable loan, once the commitments are in—otherwise you could nip the sale in the budding stages. Given time, buyers and sellers often change their minds about what they will do.

An alternative under the above circumstances would be that you could accept the offer after adding the following condition: "The seller reserves the right to accept any other offer, upon giving 48 hours written notice to buyer or buyer's agent, prior to buyer's removal in writing of all contingencies to this offer." Such a contingency will serve to get some buyers off the hook. It is sometimes the only acceptable alternative for the seller, and it should almost always be included in

HOW TO NEGOTIATE

any sales agreement where the closing of the deal is subject to the sale of some other property owned by the buyer. Under these conditions, your property would remain on the market while the buyer was attempting to sell his property.

I have seen too many deals fall through because a broker just let the deal drop when the requested financing could not be obtained. The broker should always try to get the buyer and seller to reach a compromise, and particularly when attractive alternatives are available. Most brokers who prospered during the tight-money market did so by trying another method if the first attempt to put a deal together didn't work out, and then another if the second didn't work. If there is a will, there is a way, in most cases.

Other contingencies which should be watched and limited to a reasonable number of days, rather than have them apply to the entire escrow period are:

A. Subject to further inspection and approval of the property (or furniture, fixtures, leases, etc.).

B. Subject to buyer's inspection and approval of a pest control report.

C. Subject to buyer's inspection and approval of public health or building inspection reports against the property—in the event such a report exists.

D. Any other contingency which could be met in substantially fewer days than the full escrow period. If you have a 30-day escrow period and it would be expected to take more than approximately 15 days to remove any of the contingencies, then you should just let it run the whole period if necessary, in the interest of avoiding complications. The less complications, the better, so use common sense before insisting on restrictions which might do more harm than good. Sometimes, the other party to the transaction will be more agreeable to making certain concessions and accepting terms and conditions other than those requested if he is not forced into a corner—the more a particular point is brought up and hashed over, the more it is likely to stick in the minds of the parties involved. Sometimes, you can get further by making light of some fairly serious matters.

5. Get the buyer while he's hot

When counteroffering to any offer submitted by a prospective buyer, always insert the clause: "The seller reserves the right to accept any other offer prior to receiving notification in writing of acceptance of this counteroffer." Also, always specify the number of days that your counteroffer is good, after which time you will not be bound by its terms.

6. Don't be an interest hog

When you are selling and it is necessary for you to carry back a relatively short term second or third loan for the buyer, don't try to squeeze the interest rate. It is all right to ask for a high rate, but you should not get hung up on it. Reducing the due-date of the loan may be more important to you, as a seller, than raising the interest rate.

The difference between one or two percentage points usually will not add up to much, and your insistence on a high rate may turn the buyer off or discourage him to the point where it would be difficult for you to get a good price or other favorable terms. An exception, however, is that the terms of the loan are important if you plan to use the loan in-lieu-of, or in addition to, a down payment to purchase another property. In that case, the interest rate could be important, but obtaining the minimum number of years before the due date of the loan may be more important. Even more important to such a loan, is that it should contain a "due on sale" clause, if at all possible. Though, again, the importance of the sale and getting a good price will usually outweigh the need for minor changes in the terms of secondary financing.

7. Don't always insist on an all-cash sale

While it is obviously desirable to receive all cash for your property, your insistence on this, and particularly bringing up the subject before you have hooked an interested party, can make the sale of the property very difficult, indeed. It will also most likely lower the ultimate selling price, since you will have narrowed your field of buyers to a fairly small percentage of the market. Most properties are sold with some kind of secondary financing.

Even if you must have all cash, it will sometimes be to your advantage to accept a good offer involving some secondary financing, then sell the loan you are carrying back, in order to make up the balance of the cash needed. By getting a higher price for the property, you may be able to discount the loan you carry back and still come out with the cash you need. But, be careful of a third loan if you are planning to sell it. Essentially, it may be just as good as a second loan, but a third would be more difficult to sell, requiring a higher percentage discount.

Make sure that proper wording is used when you accept an offer on your property which calls for your carrying back secondary financing. There are many acceptable ways to phrase the proposal, but there are certain key words or phrases that must be included in order to protect you. The note and deed of trust will be drawn up by the escrow company, but the buyer can hold you to the basic terms of your sales agreement. So make sure that the terms of the sales agreement specify the dollar amount of the note, the interest rate, the due date, the amount of the monthly payments, and that the note is to be secured by a deed of trust on the subject property (specify street address or some such identification), and whether the note is to be due in full on sale or transfer of the property.

If it is important that the buyer secure the financing from the lender of the existing first loan in order for you to avoid paying a prepayment penalty, then you must specify in the sales agreement that the loan is to be assumed by or that any new loan is to be secured with, the same lender. However, never make these demands at the time you are listing your property for sale, since some buyers will want to try other sources of financing, and you won't want to discourage them before giving them a chance to get interested in your property. In fact, if the buyer is willing to pay enough for your property, you can afford to pay the prepayment penalty.

While it is good to try to arrange the terms so that a prepayment penalty can be avoided, it is not always a good idea to insist on its avoidance when you see it is going to kill the deal. The net proceeds you will receive from the sale are the most important thing. Also, while many prospective buyers will have their pet sources of financing, they usually will not be able to obtain the loan they want from that source and, in the end, will very often come back to the existing lender anyway. But if you had scared them off before they realized that they could not go their preferred route, then you would have lost a sale and limited the field of buyers.

Other important conditions that apply whether you are the buyer or seller:

—Never rely on the oral promise or agreement between yourself and the broker or the other principal to the transaction. If it is important, make sure that it is spelled out in writing in the sales agreement or a binding addendum.

—Keep in mind that the money market changes from month to month. Although any active broker should be fairly well-versed on the prevailing money market, the chances are that he will not be. Some brokers simply are not that alert to begin with, and then the constant changes do make it a problem to keep up to date.

—Don't sign any commitment to buy or sell until you have had at least a few hours, and preferably overnight, to think it over; unless you know for sure what you wanted to do and have not been persuaded by sales talk.

—As a buyer or seller, if you want the broker to cut his commission in order to make the price acceptable to you, it is often best to set the stage but not to bring up the subject directly. Brokers are much less likely to cut their commissions when asked, than when you just hold the price at a reasonable distance from what the other principal will agree upon, so that the broker could cut his commission by that amount and have a deal with a reasonable earned commission. This will not always work, however, so once the broker is convinced that he has reached an impasse and he still does not offer to give up part of his commission, you can either bring up the subject or go ahead and adjust your position so the deal can be consummated.

Usually, I cannot say that I recommend trying to get the broker to cut his commission. He has supposedly done a job and he should be paid for it. However, there may be times when you have reached the limit of your price adjustment and it is up to the broker to decide whether to let it fall apart or to take a lesser commission and close the deal.

But do not take the position that a broker is obligated to cut his commission. It is unfair and it may not be in your best interest, in the long run. If a broker doesn't get sufficient compensation for his work, he may not work as hard for you the next time.

15

Getting Started with Little or No Cash

How can I invest in real estate when I have little or no cash? You do not need any large sum of cash on hand in order to make real estate investments, but it is almost essential that you have at least a few hundred dollars, and preferably more, of course. The more cash you have, the better choice of investments and investment methods you will have. But, again, a small amount will do if necessary.

If you do not have access to at least a small amount of cash, and if getting a nest egg together, however small it might be, is a problem for you then your best course is to set up an austerity program to curb your spending to bare essentials. You will be surprised how much money you are spending on non-essentials, once you start your savings program.

If you have difficulty in sticking to a savings program, take along with you at all times a piece of paper on which to write the expenditure of every single item, even if only a dime. It will be very helpful, and it will be interesting to look back on after a few weeks. I did this once, not to budget myself, but to find out how much I was spending each month so I could set up a reasonable budget that would not be too stringent or unworkable. It worked so well, in fact, that I didn't have to set up a budget at all. Every time I started to purchase something, even a very small item, I would think of putting it on the list and then it would occur to me that the purchase was totally unnecessary. The list had quite an inhibiting influence on spending.

Also, when I decided to save money for the purchase of my first real estate venture, I discovered all sorts of very inexpensive foods that were just super, and for about three months I had a delightful time discovering delectable dishes which cost almost nothing in comparison to my usual grocery budget. In addition to being quite palatable, some of the most inexpensive foods are the most nourishing.

Eating out is strictly a no-no-no when you are trying to save money in a hurry—just watch how much you can save by keeping your coffee breaks to just that. It will also be good for your health and your waist line. There are also many forms of free entertainment available. And, I dare say, you will find the change refreshing.

If you start your austerity program as described above, you should have enough cash saved to make your initial investment by the time you are able to familiarize yourself with the market, which in any event, should be done before you start your investment program.

THE IMPORTANCE OF GOOD CREDIT

The one thing you will find almost more necessary than cash is good credit. If you don't have good credit, or any credit rating at all because you have always paid cash for everything, then start immediately to establish a good rating. If you don't have any credit cards, get at least two as soon as possible. This may be a problem for some people, since it could be tempting to make unnecessary purchases just when you are supposed to be saving as much as possible. But the cards will be invaluable as a source of delayed payment purchasing power, in buying material you will be needing to spruce up your property. Generally, you should have at least three reasonably current credit references when you go to purchase real estate or to borrow money to make improvements.

One of the best ways to build your credit is to borrow from your bank, even if a very small amount and all you plan to do is put the money in the savings account. Then, pay the loan off in monthly installments, making each payment a little ahead of schedule.

Even if you have substantial funds at your disposal, you will need to work with other people's money in order to obtain an attractive leverage position.

An important consideration, which will affect your ability to secure real estate loans and other needed financing, is your job stability. If you are planning to change jobs, it may be advisable for you to postpone the change until after you have made an anticipated real estate investment, particularly if you are not too strong in other aspects of the credit picture. Lenders sometimes turn applicants down on credit applications when the applicant has been employed in his position only a short time. However, policy varies greatly from one lender to another, so remember to try more than one if it becomes a problem. Generally, during the course of your real estate dealings, it would prove fruitful for you to follow the well-known proverb, "If at first you don't succeed, try, try again." Don't be a quitter.

SOURCES OF CASH OR ITS EQUIVALENT

Shortly after the purchase of my first real estate investment and before it was re-sold, I discovered another property I wanted to purchase. But having just exhausted all my resources to make the first investment, I was in no position to purchase a second one. So what I did was to borrow $1,000 from a friend who had just made some easy money on a real estate deal. That $1,000 constituted the whole of the down payment and closing costs to acquire the second property. It was purchased on an Agreement of Sale (or Contract of Sale) with a clause stipulating that I must completely remodel the house within three months so a good loan could be obtained and title transferred to my name. The house was quite a sight as it had been vacant for eight years. With no money to remodel, but with a fair paying job and good credit, I charged most of the material necessary for the remodeling. I paid cash out of my monthly income for the electrical and plumbing labor costs, which are more difficult to charge than some others.

Actually, it took me four months to complete the remodeling, after which I was able to secure a new first loan for the full amount I had paid for the house. I sold the house a few months later, paid my friend his $1,000 and with the proceeds left over I was able to purchase a three-unit building and have money left over for remodeling.

It might sound risky, to go out on a limb with no resources to fall back on, but when you have nothing, which was basically my situation at the time, there seemed to be little that could be lost, yet a lot could be gained. Actually, at the time I did not feel that there was any problem in living up to my commitments. But if you are a bit more conservative, then you may want to wait until your savings permit you to proceed with a little more reserve.

I have a good friend who jokingly tells what he went through when he purchased his first house. He was single and yet purchased a large three-story, nine-room house. It was in excellent condition, so no work was required, but he only had enough furniture to fill two rooms, and even that had not yet arrived from New York, where he had previously lived. He had depleted his cash reserves and severely strained his credit in his efforts to raise the down payment and closing costs. But since he wanted to rent some of the rooms to people on a share rental basis, he needed furniture. What he did was to show the house to prospective renters and when they asked about the furniture, he would tell them it was coming in from New York, neglecting to say, of course, that it was only enough furniture for the living room and his own bedroom. He required a $100 security deposit plus the first month's rent of $90 from each tenant in advance. Then with the $190 received from each tenant he would rush out and purchase an inexpensive, but fairly nice, used bed and dresser. In that way, and with the proceeds from the three or four monthly rentals, he was able to furnish the house completely in a short period of time, while telling the tenants that, for some unexplained reason, his furniture was arriving a little at a time. This type of thing may not be your bag, but you can see how, with a little imagination and ingenuity, a person can get a lot done with very little cash in hand.

There are as many ways as there are people wanting to do them. Such as getting the real estate broker to lend his commission to apply toward the down payment. Or perhaps you could borrow on your life insurance. Or take an option on the property, or a lease option; or purchase on Agreement of Sale, all of which cut down considerably on the cash outlay required. I am sure you will think of other cash substitutes, once you get into the swing of things. (For a more detailed discussion of this subject, see Chapter 16.)

ACQUIRING PROPERTY UNDER A LEASE-OPTION

Many times, it is possible to take possession of real estate, with most of the rights of an owner, under a lease-option agreement. This means that you lease the property for one or more years, with the option to purchase at any time during that period at a specified price and terms.

It is a good idea, as always in purchasing real estate, to try to arrange any secondary financing which the owner is agreeing to carry back so that it will not be due on sale. In this way, you may transfer the second loan to the new buyer, thus probably making the property more salable and making it easier for you to get all cash for the equity you have built up. Such an arrangement can be very valuable to the investor who has very little cash to lay out.

By taking a lease-option and thus obtaining the right to purchase the property if you so choose, you may actually be in a better position than you would be if you had purchased it. That is because with a lease-option which makes some provision for your right as a lessee to make changes, you can make improvements and redecorate the property, the costs of which can be charged and paid monthly. Then, when you are successful in obtaining a buyer for the property at a price which would net you an acceptable profit, you simply exercise your option to purchase at the lower pre-determined price. Usually, a one-year lease-option should be quite enough time in which to handle your end of the transaction successfully, though it would be advisable to try for a longer lease period, just in case... The longer period would give

GETTING STARTED WITH LITTLE OR NO CASH 155

you some leeway, in the event you misjudged the marketability of the property. And, since you would have very little cash tied up in the property, it would be worth waiting for the right buyer or for inflation to bring you a profit. Also, a portion of the monthly lease payments may be applied toward the purchase price when the option is exercised.

There is no set pattern as to how much of the lease payments would apply toward the purchase price. It is strictly a matter of agreement which should be spelled out in the lease. You just bargain for the best acceptable arrangements you can get. Sometimes, in order to get a portion of the lease payments to apply on the purchase price, you must pay an amount larger than would be required under a normal lease. It is a way of forced savings.

Another advantage of the lease-option is that, in the event the property is totally unsalable for a price which would benefit you, you need not exercise your option and you would only lose your remodeling and decorating expenses, which should be kept as low as possible anyway, considering that your talents are as yet unproved.

As a rule—especially for the beginner—the property which lends itself best to the lease-option method of handling is the single family dwelling or a two-or three-unit building. It would be a great savings for you to occupy the house or one of the income units while redecorating it, in order to avoid paying double residence costs. You will sometimes be able to get the owner to defer commencement of the monthly installments for a month or more, usually depending a great deal on the condition of the property and how much difficulty the owners have been experiencing with repair bills, vacancies, bad tenants, etc.

Which leads us to the type of property which is most easily obtained on the lease-option method; and that is the property which is listed for sale, rather than for rent, and has been on the market for a considerable length of time. It will probably be vacant or with existing low rents, and usually in need of considerable repair and decorating. Owners of such properties will often be open to any reasonable suggestion that would take the property off their hands and relieve them of the financial responsibility, with the implied promise of a later sale. Do not let brokers discourage you from making an offer on the lease-option basis. Many brokers, partially out of ignorance, will tell you that the owners will not consider such a proposition since they do not know what the owner will consider. But a motive the broker might have for discouraging such an arrangement is that he would not normally obtain his selling commission unless, and until, you exercise your option to purchase, although he would normally be able to get a leasing commission at once.

On your first lease option, at least, be sure to use the services of an attorney to make sure you have an air-tight deal. This is of particular importance because the owner may get wind of your projected sale and, unless you have an unbreakable lease, he could decide to squelch your deal when he sees that you are selling at a higher price. After you have successfully completed your first lease-option, you may be able to use the transaction as an example for drawing up papers for subsequent deals.

THE COST OF SECURING AN OPTION TO PURCHASE

With $100.00 I once obtained a 120-day option to purchase a 125 acre ranch at a price of $125,000. I also obtained excellent terms and a one-time transfer clause for the financing which was being carried back by the seller. This was done, also, with the seller having the services of an experienced real estate attorney, though he was a bit senile. In fact, I am quite sure that the only reason I was able to get my deal through was because the seller's attorney was so difficult, making so many unusual demands on the seller's behalf, that no other interested party had the patience, persistence, or flexibility to cope with the situation. In fact, I'm not quite sure how I got through it. The seller was not difficult at all—the attorney kept changing things against the seller's will, but since the attorney had represented the seller's family for several generations the seller would not go against his advice. I have several reasons for telling this story, not the least of which is to stress the fact that some of the best deals will be available to you on terms you can live with—if you will not stick to hard and fast rules when an alternative would be just as good—only because the owner or his advisors are so difficult that they scare off most prospective purchasers.

I had planned to exercise my option and hold the property for appreciation, but it turned out that during the option period someone came to me out of the blue, it seemed—actually he was referred to me by a friend of the person who owned the ranch—and offered me $15,000 more than I had paid for the property. I decided to take it, since I had subsequently located an apartment building I wanted to purchase, which I could not have done without selling the ranch. The seller balked on closing the deal and tried to stall me into eternity. But the deal was apparently air-tight so we eventually closed it, after I hired an attorney and threatened a law suit. The financing carried back by the seller, which was so good that it was the best selling feature of the deal, was transferred to the new owner. That experience proves another point—that patience and persistence can be next to "goldliness!"

It is impossible to say how much money you will need for any particular option agreement. It could range from $1.00 on up. The maximum you should be willing to put on an option would depend on many things, such as:

How firm your plans are to exercise the option;
The amount of profit you plan to make; and
The length of the option.

But remember that whatever option money you put up is forfeited in the event you do not exercise your option within the terms of the agreement.

I, personally, have not worked much with options. One reason is that as a Realtor, under California law, I could be obligated to divulge my plans to the seller. And it is hard to imagine most sellers agreeing to sell a property when they learn that the buyer plans to sell for substantially more than the purchase price. But the use of options can be very convenient, as well as beneficial.

Some investors use options to tie up properties that they feel are marketable at a higher price. Then they attempt to obtain a firm commitment from a buyer at a higher price. If they are successful, they sign the agreement to sell the property, subject to the close of the escrow which encompasses their original option to purchase. (If no escrow exists, it can be opened by simply telephoning the title or escrow company.) That, or a similar arrangement, is necessary since you should not sign a totally binding agreement to sell property which is not yet recorded in your name. But you are safe in signing such an agreement that is properly worded so that you will have an out, in the event, for any reason, you are unable to obtain title to the property.

Under such an arrangement, title is usually transferred simultaneously to you and then to your buyer. It is referred to as a "double escrow." In drawing up the option agreement, the services of a competent attorney would be advisable, in order to protect yourself against wrongful handling and to insure that the seller cannot back out if he discovers what you are doing.

THE AGREEMENT OF SALE

The agreement of sale gained wide acceptance after the 1966 credit crunch which made the interest rate and loan fees on new loans prohibitive for many purchasers. By using the agreement of sale, the property could be physically transferred, giving the new holder virtually all the rights of ownership, plus the benefit of the low interest rate on the existing loan. And since title to the property does not transfer under the agreement of sale until all the terms of the agreement have been met, which can mean a time span of from weeks to years, the lending institutions were prevented from increasing the interest rates or charging loan fees until title transferred.

The agreement of sale worked, in principle, because real estate is technically not considered sold until title to the property is transferred—the agreement is an agreement to purchase the property at a specified price and terms, upon the performance by both parties of all the terms of the agreement. A provision is included in most mortgage or deed of trust agreements with lending institutions which allows the lender to demand payment in full or to alter the terms of the loan in the event the property is sold. But under the agreement of sale, reputedly the property is not yet sold, thus preventing the lender from calling the loan (demanding payoff or performance in accordance with his demands) or changing the terms of the loan until such time as title is transferred to the new owner. However, since the agreement of sale came into wide usage, some lenders have changed their mortgage and deed of trust agreements to extend their rights not only to the sale or the property, but to any transfer by such means as the agreement of sale.

When the agreement of sale ran into trouble through lender objections, a new device was used to serve the same purpose and at the same time avoid the lender's interference. That was the lease-option agreement. When the lease-option was used solely for the purpose of delaying transfer of title to the property, the buyer would usually put up as option money an amount equivalent to what his down payment would be if the purchase had actually been consummated. Such a move is quite safe with a properly worded agreement, since the buyer would obviously intend to exercise his option before the expiration date, hopefully at a time when financing arrangements had improved, and both the buyer and seller were satisfied. The buyer would have his property and the seller would have his down payment and could take over the property in the event the buyer failed to live up to the terms of the option agreement. Bear in mind, though, that this practice was most widely used during a slow market when buyers were hard to come by and sellers were often unable to sell their property under any other arrangements.

Aside from trying to prolong the arrangement of finances for the property in order to obtain more favorable interest rates and loan fees, the most common use of the agreement of sale is to delay temporarily financing a property, because the buyer's down payment is not sufficient to qualify for the necessary loan, since all financing requires a specified percentage of the purchase price as the initial down payment. VA financing is a possible exception, but even with the VA, substantial closing costs are often required to come out of the buyer's pocket, whereas with the agreement of sale, all closing costs can be put off until the buyer gets a loan and takes title to the property—even prorations of taxes and insurance can be delayed if agreeable to the seller.

Many times the agreement of sale is desirable in order to give the buyer time to do the necessary remodeling or decorating to put the property in good showing condition so a reasonable loan can be obtained. This can benefit both the buyer and seller, since obtaining a low percentage loan due to the poor condition of the property would usually mean that the seller would be required to carry back a second loan. Whereas, after the redecorating is completed, the obtainable loan would often be increased sufficiently to eliminate the need for secondary financing, plus the fact that the rate of interest would be lower after the property was put in better showing condition.

OTHER IMPORTANT POINTS TO CONSIDER

It is of particular importance at this juncture in your endeavours that you select the types of property which are easily sold, so you will not get stuck with a property for a long time—since it is assumed that you would not have other funds with which to move on to another investment while you were waiting for the sale of the first.

So, if some of this information is repetitive, it is because of the particular importance at this stage. It is never desirable, of course, to get stuck with a property which is difficult or impossible to sell, but at this point such failure would not only dull your enthusiasm for further ventures, but it would slow your progress considerably. So at this point, for the most part, it would be best to stick to a single family, a duplex (flats), or at most a three-unit building—they sell more rapidly than other buildings.

Buildings with four or more units are somewhat less easily sold, as a rule, since they are a little more than most prospective purchasers who want to live in one unit and rent out the others would want to cope with in the way of rental property at their doorstep. At the same time, four-to six-unit buildings are not enough units in one parcel to attract most prospects who are looking for strictly investment property. There are many exceptions, of course, and many four- to six-unit buildings sell quite readily. But for a beginner, it would be best not to add the additional burden until such time as you can hold the property, if necessary, and at the same time proceed with other investments. Also, avoid buildings with stores, or other commercial aspects. It is not uncommon for commercial property to experience long delays in either renting or selling. Residential property, though, can always be rented at a reasonable price, and sales are far more easy to come by, as a whole.

All three of the methods of acquiring property discussed earlier in this chapter have the initial advantage of avoiding most or all your closing costs until such time as you take title to the property. This means less cash outlay to take over the property and it gives you time to save up any additional cash required for the down payment. These methods of obtaining property often have another important advantage for the beginner who may be operating on a rather small profit margin —that of avoiding the normal buying and selling escrow costs in the event the investor sells the property at the time he is exercising his option-to-purchase under the provisions of a double-escrow. In such instances, the buyer would pay for the loan fees on the new loan, plus other normal closing costs, and the seller (from whom the property was purchased) would pay any prepayment penalty on the existing loan, in the absence of an agreement to the contrary.

Cash down payment requirements vary greatly throughout the country and just as much between rival lending institutions in any given area. The best conventional loans from banks, savings and loan associations, etc., are obtainable with five percent down and a loan of 95 percent of the selling price on single-family dwellings where the buyer is to occupy the house, but credit and income requirements are stricter for these loans. The interest rate and loan fee on a 95 percent loan are a little higher than would be required with a smaller loan. Next in line, is the 90 percent conventional loan, which operates much the same as the 95 percent loan, but with a little lower interest rate and loan fee. Some lenders will permit a five percent second loan under the 90 percent plan, which means a down payment of still only five percent, if the seller will carry back the balance on a second loan.

The next conventional loan for the single family, as well as multiple unit buildings, is the 75 percent to 80 percent loan which we have had around for a long time except that from 1966 to 1970 they were often lowered to 60 percent or 70 percent of the selling price due to the shortage of funds. Under the 75 percent to 80 percent plan, the interest rate and loan fees are a little lower than with the 90 percent loan, and most lenders will permit the buyer to have a second loan, and possibly a third. The cash down payment for the 75 percent to 80 percent conventional loans is usually a minimum of ten percent of the selling price, but it is often 15 percent and sometimes 20 percent of the selling price. These requirements vary from time to time, depending on the availability of mortgage money.

Some institutions are slower than others to change their policies, so during the transition period, shopping around will reveal the lender who has the most favorable rate. Also, lenders change their policies on the percentage of the selling price they will lend, as well as their interest rates and loan fees, depending on the availability of funds and sometimes depending on the condition of the particular lender's loan portfolio. So the policy of several lenders in any area does not necessarily reflect the policy of all others.

It is usually best to figure on holding your property at least six months in order to take advantage of the long-term capital gains, unless you have enough deductions to offset the gain, or unless you have another investment opportunity in mind which requires the funds from the sale of your property, and which would benefit you more than holding out for a long-term gain.

The idea is to keep your capital working. It is sometimes more important to go on to another investment than to hold back because of taxes. Too many people lose track of what action is preferable because they get too obsessed with avoiding income taxes. However, income taxes are usually an important factor when any substantial gain is involved. So if you have a close count in figuring what you think is a six-months period, be sure to check it out before you close the escrow. Also, there is proposed legislation at this time which could change the holding period requirement for real estate, in order to qualify for long term capital gains treatment.

The last advice in this chapter is for those of you who might be tempted to go on a spending spree when you reaceive the proceeds from your first few sales. It is important that you hold back on elevating your standard of living for a while, in order to reinvest your capital. The person, or organization, who does not put a considerable portion of his business earnings back into the business will not progress very rapidly. And the less funds you had to begin with, the more important it is to put the earnings back to work. So, remember that a little restraint on your spending at this point will make possible a far more rapid development and the opportunity for a much better standard of living a little later on.

In fact, after one successful investment using any one of the three above-described principles, you should be financially able to move on to the practice outlined in the next chapter—unless, of course, one of these three methods is again best suited for the investment you have chosen.

16

Minimum Cash Investment

The term "minimum cash investment" is intended primarily to cover the investment with conventional financing, such as banks or savings and loan institutions. As a rule, they require a cash down payment from 5 percent to 25 percent of the selling price, with an average requirement of from 10 percent to 20 percent. It is the 10 percent to 15 percent down payment you will most likely be working with in the beginning when your cash reserves are likely to be low. The difference between the lender's loan commitment and your cash down payment must be made up by secondary financing, normally carried back by the seller. So, for the most part, the cash down payment will be a minimum of ten percent of the selling price on properties which meet the specifications outlined earlier in this book, relating to good investment prospects. Most buildings with five or more units will require a minimum 15 percent down payment. These requirements may vary in different parts of the country, but they are influenced more by the availability of mortgage money at any given time.

VA and FHA loans will not be covered at this time, since they are not very often available for the type of properties under discussion here.

HOW TO GENERATE CASH FOR THE DOWN PAYMENT

All the cash down payment need not necessarily come out of your pocket. There are many ways of generating cash or cash credits or substitutes when you are purchasing real estate. These sources can assist in lowering your actual cash outlay to a very nominal figure. Some of the information which pertains here is covered in Chapter 12 under "Prime Sources of Financing." In addition, the following suggestions may be helpful in raising the down payment for some of your ventures.

One of the simplest ways to obtain funds is to get the broker to lend you his commission. Ideally, you would have an arrangement with the broker as to what portion of his commission he will lend you before you make your commitment to purchase. But since many brokers are reluctant to lend their commissions, it may be necessary for you to do some maneuvering to get them to go along with you.

As a broker, I was subjected to "the treatment" many times. Although I usually stated very flatly and firmly, when the subject came up, that I would not lend my commission, the truth is that I usually would have if it was a matter of losing the deal or taking a note for my commission. However, some brokers are stubborn and foolish, and will actually see deals go down the drain time and time again by refusing to take their commission in a note. If this happens, and you need the commission in order to swing the deal, then get yourself another broker—or if you use a diplomatic approach in letting the broker know your determination, you may get his cooperation.

Probably the best way to get the broker to go along with lending the commission, when it has not been previously arranged, is to make your offer without mention of this need. Then, at a crucial moment in the negotiations, bring up the fact that you do not have enough funds to purchase the property—in other words, you leave the impression that you are ready to give up. If he doesn't offer his assistance at this point, you could then do a little more prodding or even bring up the subject directly. It is really not fair to the seller or the broker, but you can actually wait until the negotiations have been successfully completed to bring up this need, but in this case you would need to have some sort of contingency clause which would give you the right to drop the deal.

Moreover, though most locations will have established by custom who normally pays certain closing costs, such as the loan fee, title insurance and escrow fees (the latter two are included as one fee in some areas, while treated as separately in others), in effect they can be negotiated between the buyer and seller, regardless of the local custom. Trying to negotiate these fees against the normal practice can sour your deal, however, so it is not always wise to press for the maximum advantage, unless it is crucial to your ability to finance the transaction.

In the event there is a definite custom that either buyer or seller pays a certain closing cost, then the simple wording "buyer (or seller) agrees to pay normal closing costs" should be sufficient. In the absence of an established custom, then, who is to pay each item of closing costs should be spelled out in your purchase agreement.

Put your income tax money to work. If you normally pay your income taxes quarterly because you are self-

MINIMUM CASH INVESTMENT

employed or have outside income, then an easy and relatively painless method of obtaining investment capital would be to postpone payment of the quarterly estimated tax until you file your tax return. This gives you the benefit of up to one year's use of the funds at a nominal cost—and the penalty for not filing and paying your quarterly taxes is six percent per annum on the unpaid portion. That is a very inexpensive loan. In addition, the investment you make with the money would give you a considerable tax deduction which would, in turn, lower the total tax bill, even after adding on the six-percent penalty.

I once knew a doctor who went even further toward solving his problem of not having enough investment capital. He was in a very high tax bracket and had no tax deductions. He had not thought much about paying the high taxes, since he had enough left over to live comfortably. . . until he got a divorce and had to start paying alimony, which left him short of funds for even a moderate standard of living. Then he realized something had to be done. So he stopped paying his quarterly income taxes and went to the bank and borrowed as much money as he could on his personal signature. With the combined funds, he purchased a large apartment building with the bare minimum down payment. As a result of this maneuver, when his taxes came due the next year, his tax obligation was substantially reduced due to the large write-off the apartment building provided. Then, with the money he saved on taxes, he was able to pay off a substantial portion of the personal loan the first year alone. So, what he did was to take money that he would have normally paid in income taxes and put it to work, not only building up equity in a real estate investment, but also reducing his income tax obligation for the near as well as the long term.

There are many other creative methods of temporarily

obtaining funds for investments, though I cannot recommend all of them. One such method I have suspected some youthful investors of using is to borrow from the Federal Government under the student loan provision, some of which is tax free until the student completes school. Another is, after you have acquired a property, it is sometimes possible to get improvement loans, the funds from which can actually be applied to purchase other real estate, rather than to perform the work for which the loan was obtained. For small improvement loans, lenders seldom follow through to the extent of checking to see that the work was performed. If they were inclined to do that, you should be able to tell when you applied for the loan and before you made it final. While I have not done this, and I can't recommend it, I know that it has been done by others. And in the few cases where I did obtain an improvement loan, I could have used the money for other purposes and the lenders would never have known.

Another way of generating cash, for example, is when you specify in your offer to purchase that the seller is to pay for any work specified by a pest control operator, or for any other improvements or repairs. Rather than specify that the owner is to pay for such work, word your statement so that you will be credited in escrow for the amount of the work required. Your broker should have a standard phrase, but a small change might be necessary in order to get the desired results. This approach will not help if the lending institution insists on the work actually being completed prior to close of escrow, or that the funds be held in escrow until the work is completed. But in the absence of the lender requiring that the work be performed, receiving a credit for the amount of repairs would sometimes add substantially to your cash position; since, in effect, if you are credited in escrow with the amount of the cost of the work that the seller has agreed to pay, then your closing costs would be reduced by a like amount.

For example, let's assume the work required under such a provision would cost $500 and that the lender did not restrict the loan commitment in regards to the required work; you could then apply that $500 toward your down payment or closing costs. I know of a case where the buyer was able to get a credit of $7,500, in this manner, on the purchase of an apartment building. In that case, the work required by the report was mostly superficial, involving partitions and other such non-structural work. So the work was never performed, even though the buyer got the full credit in escrow, which amounted to the larger portion of the down payment.

HOW MUCH SHOULD I ALLOW FOR CLOSING COSTS?

Closing costs vary so much from one deal to the next that it is virtually impossible to arrive at a meaningful figure in general discussions. But the following information will make it possible for you to figure roughly what your closing costs will be, once you have selected an investment. Your broker can, and should, help in this area, but do not accept any total closing cost figure your broker gives you without first having gone over it item by item—to make sure the figures have not been understated by a significant amount. Even a well-intended broker may not go over the closing costs closely enough to be accurate. And then, there are brokers who will intentionally understate the closing costs in an effort to make the deal sound more attractive to you. When the day of truth comes and your closing costs are double what you had anticipated, he knows you will come up with the money somehow, even if it means his lending it to you. I have seen buyers in an awful mess, with staggering closing costs that were far beyond anything they might have dreamed. Usually, it was the result of the broker's having picked a rough figure out of the air based on most other transactions, rather than actually figuring the itemized costs involved in that particular deal.

In a standard escrow, the closing costs will include many, but not necessarily all, of the following charges:

1. Title insurance.

2. Escrow Fee—if not included in the title insurance fee. In some areas the buyer pays both the title insurance and the escrow fee. In many areas these fees are split 50-50 between the buyer and seller. I do not know of any area where the seller pays the entire cost of title insurance and escrow fees.

3. Proration of taxes.

4. Proration of rents, lease deposits, and security deposits.

5. Proration of interest—The first payment of a new first loan is always at least 30 days after close of escrow, and it is often up to 45 or 50 days after closing. Since the interest on most real estate loans is paid in arrears, rather than in advance, each payment will include interest for the 30 days preceding the due date of that payment. So, the interest on any days over and above 30 will be charged in escrow to the buyer. Also—and note this—when you get a loan commitment from a lending institution, inquire as to whether the interest is charged in advance or in arrears. A few lenders charge interest in advance, in which case you, as buyer, would also be required to pay the interest in escrow for the

first 30 days of the loan. If your broker is not aware of the existence of such lender policies, then he may mislead you by saying that there is no difference. But after you have received a commitment you should inquire as to the particular lender's policy, in the event the extra 30 days interest in escrow would create a cash shortage.

If you are assuming an existing loan, as opposed to securing a new one, you (as the buyer) should actually receive credit from the seller to cover interest from the date of the last payment up to the date of closing; unless the interest is paid in advance, in which case you would owe the seller for the number of days from the date of closing to the due date of the next payment. The title or escrow company should figure all this out, so you need not worry, except where it concerns your budget.

6. Loan fee—The local custom on average transactions will determine who is to pay this fee, unless otherwise clarified in negotiations. Loan fees on conventional loans are normally between one and two percent of the amount of the loan; however, the fee can be as low as zero, in rare instances, and it is not unusual for the loan fee to run 2½ to 4 percent on loans in excess of 80 percent of the selling price. And in recent years, some loan fees, more notably **VA** and **FHA** (the latter of which must be paid by the seller—a requirement of FHA), have gone as high as five to six percent of the selling price. The loan fees, like interest, will go up and down along with the availability of funds. Either primary or secondary loans carried back by the seller do not normally have loan fees, though a few sellers will demand one.

7. Insurance—As a buyer, you will usually be required to pay at least one-year's insurance prior to escrow closing; except when the seller is carrying back the first loan or when you are assuming existing insurance, in which case, you may be able to pay one month or one quarter at a time, or pay the prorated portion of the amount already paid by the seller. In the latter case, the seller would get a credit in escrow. Insurance costs may be considerably different for each owner, depending on the coverage required or desired.

8. Impound account—In recent years many lenders have started requiring that an impound account be set up with them from which they will pay the property taxes and insurance when they are due; although you will still be required to pay certain prorations in escrow, as described in number 6 above. Added to the monthly payments will be an amount sufficient to accumulate funds for payment of taxes and insurance.

The initial deposit to the impound account required at closing of escrow will vary considerably, depending on the time of year you close the transaction. You can determine roughly how much the initial deposit to the impound account will be by figuring the number of payments you will have on the loan before a tax installment is due and subtracting that figure from six (or 12 if taxes are billed in one installment); then multiply the number you get through the computation by the dollar amount of what one-month's taxes and insurance on the property would be. The figure you arrive at should be the approximate initial deposit required to the impound account, except that when the escrow closing date is 60 days or less from the date the taxes are due, the full amount of the next tax installment may be required prior to close of escrow.

Don't forget to figure on any credit to which you may be entitled (from the seller) in the event your escrow closing date is before the period to which you have been charged for taxes. If you have difficulty in following this procedure, just figure approximately 60 days taxes and 60 days insurance and that will be close enough for a rough figure as to the required contribution to the impound account.

Sometimes, although lenders do have policies they normally adhere to, it is possible to talk them into waiving the trust fund, thus saving you considerable closing costs; though it is only a temporary reprieve, of course, since the taxes must be paid within a few months in any case.

9. Appraisal fee—Most lenders have an appraisal fee of from $40 to $100, but in some areas they do not charge you the fee unless you accept their commitment.

10. There are miscellaneous closing costs which would usually be a minimum total of $25 and a maximum total of $100 for a property under $50,000.

With all the above points in mind, you can readily see how closing costs vary so much, depending on so many factors. It may look overwhelming, but if you take the items one at a time and check them out, it will be relatively easy to figure. Actually, your broker should do all this for you if you ask him, but it is important that you have a fair understanding of what to expect so you can double-check his figures in the event you expect to be operating on a tight budget.

WHAT TYPE OF PROPERTY SHOULD I START WITH?

The type of property you should select at this point in your investment program will depend a great deal on whether you will have access to additional funds for further investments if you hold, rather than sell, your next investment. If you are likely to need the funds from the sale of the property in order to do any more investing within a year or so, then it is important that you select the type of property that can be easily sold—such as the single-family dwelling to three-unit buildings. If possible, at least one of the units should contain a minimum of five (and preferably six) rooms. If the building is a house, it should have a minimum of three bedrooms, or an easy solution for you to add or convert it to three bedrooms. The reason for the three-bedroom requirement is that most purchasers of houses want at least three bedrooms and two baths, and anything less will often prove less salable, unless you are working with a house which is priced near the bottom of the market.

With two-and three-unit buildings, two bedrooms are often adequate, though a third in at least one unit would be a big asset. The size of the other unit, or units, may not be too important. The thing to be concerned with is having a product that will meet the needs of the majority of the prospective purchasers. And when you get below the space I have outlined, the number of potential buyers is reduced to a fairly small percentage of the total market force. However, since everything is relative, if you get a good enough deal on a building that does not have the preferred amount of space, it may still be a desirable investment, since you could in turn offer it for sale at an attractive price. But don't try to compare the value of the one-bedroom flat or duplex with that of

MINIMUM CASH INVESTMENT   177

a two-or three-bedroom flat or duplex—just as you would not compare the value of a two-bedroom house with that of a house with three or more bedrooms.

Beware of conversions (a building originally constructed as one or two units and later converted to two or three, etc.), unless the conversion was done well and the units have a reasonably good floor plan. A building that has been poorly converted to more units will be unpopular with the lending institutions, as well as less attractive to prospective purchasers.

If you decide that it would be desirable to hold the property for a few years, then your choice of investments could be geared a little more toward the type of income the property would produce, how well it will hold up, and the amount of money and time and effort that would be required in order to keep the property rented and in good condition. You will also need to consider some of the points brought out in earlier chapters as to whether the area itself will hold up over an extended period of time.

Your decision as to whether you should hold the property, after giving consideration to the pros and cons of holding it—including the total gain you would expect from the property over the holding period as opposed to how much you could increase that equity by investing in another property over that same period—may finally rest on whether you can refinance the property and obtain substantially the same amount of cash as you would realize by selling. That would not be at all uncommon in a case where selling would require your carrying back a second loan, or where your selling costs were otherwise unusually high.

Refinancing can also be very costly; so, before you decide, make sure you have figured the costs of refinancing as opposed to those of selling. In some cases, it will work out that by refinancing you would actually receive as much or more cash in hand than you would if you were to sell the property. In such a case, it would be foolish to sell unless there were extenuating circumstances which would make holding the property undesirable or unwise—since holding it would usually provide tax deductions, a buildup in equity, and appreciation in value. So why sell if you don't get something you can't get otherwise? This will be a point to consider for some time; but there will come a time, if you continue to expand your real estate holdings, when you may want to sell simply because you will not want to take the time to fool with renting and maintaining the property.

DOUBLING YOUR MONEY

A good rule in purchasing real estate for a quick turnover is to figure on doubling your investment within a year. That means that if you are paying $5,000 down, plus $1,000 closing costs, and plan to spend $2,000 on improvements and decorating, you should figure on selling the property within six months to a year to net you approximately $16,000 profit, which is double your cash investment. If, however, you are able to obtain some of the cash invested by some of the methods discussed earlier, such as a loan of the broker's commission, etc., you can relax your need for a profit to an amount double the amount of cash you actually took out of pocket. You will not always be accurate in your estimates, but by figuring to double your investment you will have enough leeway to insure that you make a reasonable profit.

Sometimes the profit will fall short of your expectations due to miscalculating the cost of repairs and remodeling, or due to unforeseen circumstances which may arise. But when your calculations are fairly accurate and you are able to re-

MINIMUM CASH INVESTMENT

alize the anticipated profit, or a little more, it will help to average out your profit to approximately double your investment.

The opportunities are available, make no mistake about it. But if you are unable to locate a property which satisfies the above requirements, then go ahead with the best you can find in a reasonable length of time. It may be that you are too conservative in projecting the future potential sales price. But it may also be that you are not analyzing the prospective purchases in the right way. You must look for ways to improve the properties which would not be obvious to the average looker.

Many excellent prospects are passed over by the majority of the lookers, since they do not see the potential. Sharpen your pencil and do some brainstorming for ways to enhance the value of the properties. It may take a while, but if you work at it you will soon be able to recognize "luck" when you see it. For the most part, luck is an illusive commodity. The truth is that you must be conditioned to recognize most "good luck," in order to take advantage of it—otherwise it will pass you by.

17

Ways to Protect Your Cash Investments

Regardless of how much cash you may have to invest, it is advisable to start fairly small and work up to larger investments as you learn, moving up only as rapidly as you learn. Also, don't jump from one type of investment like apartment dwellings into another such as commercial, raw land, or land development. Stick to the area you know. If you decide to branch out into other areas, be sure to do it on a small scale in the beginning until you get your bearings and learn enough about the new field to avoid some of the major pitfalls that have caused the financial ruin of many investors. A lesson here can be learned from the fact that some of the worst blunders, causing huge losses, have been incurred in development projects sponsored by large corporations which were not experienced in the real estate development business; even though they supposedly hired competent management and supervisory teams to carry out the projects. So learn from the mistakes of others when possible, and stay within the investment territory that you know and understand, or tread lightly when you venture beyond it.

TAX ADVANTAGES OF REAL ESTATE OWNERSHIP

One of the main attractions of real estate as an investment has always been the tax advantage it affords, both in the form of a tax deduction to offset other earnings and in the savings due to long term capital gains treatment when the property is sold. The lower taxes paid under the capital gains treatment afford you the opportunity to keep most of your capital working for you, rather than have it go to Uncle Sam. However, I would like to caution you not to get overly-obsessed with avoiding taxes. I have seen many investors, most often those who are in a high tax bracket, make real estate investments based more on the tax deductions the property would offer than on the overall merits of the investment. In many such cases, the income on the property is so low that the owner must pour substantial sums of money in each year in order to make ends meet—in which case the property naturally shows a good tax deduction.

I have seen investors turn down excellent investments because the income generated was so high that the tax deductions would not equal that of other properties which were poor investments, except that the latter would provide a large tax deduction. When considering all the benefits of a property as a whole, I have never understood how anyone, no matter how high his tax bracket, could come out ahead with an investment that is an actual loss (not just showing a paper loss). A gain is always better than a loss, even if 70 percent is paid out in taxes, since 30 percent would still be left over. But there is no way, through tax savings, of recouping as much as you have lost.

THE TAX FREE EXCHANGE

Where some investors lose track of their objective is in

exchanging to avoid paying tax on the gain. The exchange is a marvelous tool with which to postpone tax liability, providing it is used with discretion. In order for an exchange to be "tax free," the exchange must meet certain requirements. I will not attempt to go into all the details, since it would be too involved. But the most basic requirements of a tax free exchange are:

1. The properties exchanged must be properties of like kind.

2. The property exchanged must have been held for productive use in trade or business or for investment.

3. Gain is taxed if you receive cash or other property in addition to the exchanged property, or out of the exchange. (If the equity in your property is substantially larger than that of the one you are acquiring in an exchange, it may be that you would want to consider having your loan increased before the exchange becomes final, thus avoiding paying tax on the cash you receive.)

Where some investors go wrong is in getting obsessed with avoiding the capital gains tax. As a result they make bad investments or investments which benefit them less than if they had sold the property, paid their capital gains taxes, and then purchased a property with the cash left over.

For example, the problem occurs most often when a buyer, Mr. A, decides to purchase a property owned by Mr. X, but Mr. X delays the closing until he can find a suitable property with which to effect an exchange, owned by Mr. Y. Then Mr. X's property is exchanged for Mr. Y's property, but since Mr. Y does not want Mr. X's property, it is sold out of the exchange to Mr. A. This is all fine, except that Mr. X's new acquisition may be a mediocre or poor invest-

WAYS TO PROTECT YOUR CASH INVESTMENTS 183

ment which he may not have wanted had he not been in a rush to make the exchange.

Another thing wrong with this type of exchange is that negotiating is awkward, what with showing an exchange on paper while trying to explain to Mr. Y that he actually doesn't have to take Mr. X's property, but that it is being purchased simultaneously by Mr. A, and that he will actually receive cash for his property. Even if Mr. Y understands the exchange, the fact is that a simple offer by Mr. X to purchase his property with cash would probably have been received with greater enthusiasm by Mr. Y, with the result that Mr. Y would probably have agreed to a lower price or terms more favorable to Mr. X, than were arranged under the exchange agreement. The process of negotiating exchanges will sometimes dampen the enthusiasm of the party who wants to sell his property and does not want the property proposed for exchange, and who may have a difficult time understanding the whole transaction. Some people are bewildered by any kind of exchange.

In cases where either of the above situations exists, the loss to the party who wants to exchange his property for tax purposes may be more than could be gained by postponing the tax obligation.

Another reason why it is sometimes to the investor's advantage to sell, rather than exchange, has to do with the tax base of the property. When an exchange takes place, the tax base of the old property must be incorporated with the tax base of the newly-acquired one, thus giving a lower depreciation base from which the deduction for annual depreciation is derived. For a person who plans to have a substantially higher taxable income in the future, the larger tax deduction which would be afforded by purchasing the property, rather than acquiring it through an exchange, could change the picture—but only if he planned to keep the property for several years.

Exchanges can be valuable, and sometimes an exchange is almost essential. It's just that an exchange is not automatically an asset. So before you rush into an exchange, make sure you have considered all the consequences and that you have the transaction checked by a tax expert to make sure it qualifies for "tax free" treatment.

WILL THE IMPROVEMENTS PAY FOR THEMSELVES?

If you are planning to sell a property in the reasonably near future, then the improvements you plan to make should be geared primarily toward improving the salability of the property. Thus, the cost of any major improvements should be related to the amount that the work will increase the value of the property in terms of an increased sales price.

But when you are making improvements on a property that you plan to keep for a long time, you need to know whether the work is justified based on the amount of additional annual cash return it will generate. Assuming that the work was not essential, you would have the option of putting the money to work in another investment. Therefore, how much cash return should the improvement bring you? I have always used a rough rule of thumb that the additional income generated by an improvement should be sufficient to reimburse me in full for the expenditure within three to four years. Regular maintenance costs should not be taken into consideration here, since they must be performed in any case.

When possible, major improvements should be limited to those which would enhance the value of the property for many years, or substantially increase the rental income, and usually both. For example, updating a bathroom or kitchen would usually be a major improvement which would accomplish both goals, though decorating can and should sometimes be substituted for remodeling.

Although the cost of remodeling a kitchen or bathroom may exceed any real value in terms of the amount of additional income you can get as a result of the improvement, the added appeal of the property as a whole would usually justify such an improvement when the need is quite obvious. If the kitchen or bath is just so-so, and not terribly outdated, it may be that you should try to devise an inexpensive way to decorate, rather than remodel, so as to make them acceptable and appealing—thus avoiding a large expenditure that can't be justified in terms of a reasonable return on the cash outlay.

THE IMPORTANCE OF LEVERAGE

Leverage is still the name of the game, so don't forget to keep in mind the potential profit as related to your cash investment. There are times when what seems like an excellent buy may not be so good if the required cash investment equals a good percentage of the total purchase price, unless you have surplus cash reserves on hand which you do not plan to put to work in another investment. The question you need to ask yourself in such a situation is: Could I make a substantially larger profit with the capital if I applied it to a larger, though seemingly less attractive, investment?

PYRAMIDING

At this stage, you should be ready to stop pinching pennies and worrying about some of the minor problems, thus freeing your time and your mind for more important and productive usage. Since there are only so many hours in every day, there will come a time when, in order to progress, you must stop worrying over trivia and concentrate on broader objectives.

In order to do this, you must avoid accumulating too many small buildings. Management of most buildings which are not large enough to justify a good resident manager will consume more of your time than holding them over a long period will warrant. So start looking for larger buildings of at least 12 units each, and preferably many more.

This fits in with another point to keep in mind—that once you have accumulated substantial capital or investment equity, it is important not to put all your eggs in one basket. By dividing your funds over two or more properties, you will have more flexibility. It is important to avoid having all your funds tied up in one property, just in case it turns out to be difficult to sell. If one investment turns out to be a bomb, or less fruitful than you had anticipated, you should have other resources you can draw on in order to keep moving forward.

By pyramiding your investments, you can acquire an unbelievable amount of property in a short period of time. So, at this stage, the question is not whether you can purchase enough property, but which properties you should purchase. The properties must be serviced, managed, and properly cared for, so there may come a time when it will seem that the only solution is to hire someone to handle the detailed management of your property. However, having someone else handle your real estate investments can be a problem when your investments are such that they are more than you can comfortably handle without taking most of your time, and yet the volume is not sufficient to justify the expense of hiring competent assistance. You will need to make the decision as to whether you want to expand to the extent that you are able to hire someone to handle the day-to-day management. The answer will depend on your ultimate goal. Do you want to continue to expand and grow in the real estate investment field indefinitely, or do you just want to get situated so as to have sufficient income with which to "do your own thing."

By the time you have reached this stage, you should have learned a great deal about financing and the relative merits of sometimes refinancing and keeping property, as opposed to selling it. This subject was covered earlier, but because of the important role refinancing can play in pyramiding, I feel justified in taking it up again at this point.

Sometimes, you will be able to refinance a property and receive substantially the same amount of cash from the refinance as you could realize from a sale of the same property. That is possible because in refinancing there is no real estate commission or other selling expense, and no second note to be carried back for the buyer. Many times, I have been able to refinance properties for more than I paid for them, after completing renovation of the structures.

You should figure the cost of refinancing to determine the funds you would realize from a refinance—as opposed to a sale—taking into consideration the capital gains tax payment which a sale would necessitate. If the difference in cash to be realized is relatively small, and particularly if selling would require carrying back secondary financing, then you should consider whether it would be better to refinance and keep the property. If the property in question will pay its own way after refinancing, will build up an equity, and is likely to increase in value within the ensuing years, it's possible that selling would serve no purpose, except to relieve you of the management responsibility. That, sometimes, is the key, since some properties are headaches and require a lot of time and maintenance to keep them in good condition —in which case a sale may be justified, even though you may not receive any immediate financial benefit over and above what refinancing would do. However, if the property is relatively trouble free and is in an area where property values are expected to hold up or possibly increase, then it is quite likely that it would be wise to hold the property for some time.

If, on the other hand, the property is in an area that could possibly decline in value, or the future of which is fairly uncertain, then it would almost surely be wise to sell and go on to bigger and better things. Too often, investors sell a property just because they can see a hefty profit, when the costs of buying and selling are eating up too much of the profit. At the same time, the investor is deprived of the advantage of building up equity through holding the property over a period of time, and the advantage of the tax savings that holding the property would afford. Instead of paying out a portion of the gain in taxes, if a property is held, it will usually produce a tax savings. When the value of the equity buildup and appreciation prospects are added to the tax savings the property can produce, you may be able to see the property in a different light. But, even so, try to acquire larger properties as you progress, so you can avoid getting bogged down with management chores.

To pyramid your investments, you may either refinance or sell your property and then invest the proceeds in more or larger properties. If you refinance, rather than sell, you would still be making progress by only purchasing one other property, though you would often still be able to purchase more than one property with the refinance proceeds. So, if you either sell or refinance your properties within a year or so from the date of acquisition, it is easy to see how your holdings could mushroom into a vast empire in a relatively short period of time.

After turning over each property in this manner, you could easily and safely increase your holdings eight- to tenfold within a time span of only three or four years. And from there it can really take off, if you want to keep up the pace. In fact, even applied on a conservative scale, the results can be sensational. In what other field can control over massive wealth be acquired in a short period of time, starting from scratch?

It is the very fact that acquiring massive quantities of real estate can be so easily applied that leads me to a note of caution. It is so easy to control vast empires, by applying the principles of pyramiding, that some investors proceed with such reckless abandon that they lose sight of whether they actually own any of the wealth they are controlling. The result is that they sometimes gain control over staggering quantities of real estate, while their actual salvageable equity in those holdings is negligible. They borrow from Peter to pay Paul to cover the debt service and other operating expenses. They elevate their standards of living far beyond what their real incomes would warrant, and somewhere up there they can get caught in a bind which can be devastating. As long as the real estate market has good financing, they may be able to survive and seem to prosper. Considerable inflation in real estate prices will also bail them out, due to the extra large leverage position they maintain. If such an investor has $10,000 invested in a $200,000 property, a five-to ten-percent annual inflation in real estate prices would result in a $10,000 to $20,000 gain on the $10,000 invested. If you are enough of an adventurer, or gambler, and want to go-for-broke, that is the way to do it—

and just hope for inflation and continued good financing. If you insist on gambling at something, your odds would be better than you could get in any other form of gambling that I know of. But even if you should succeed in reaching your goal of millions in just a few years, would you know when to quit before you got wiped out by a bad market? Probably not. As a rule, the more a person gets, the more he wants, and especially when he is flying high on the magic carpet of real estate pyramiding.

But unless you purposely and knowingly choose to set out on a gambling spree, for heaven's sake be realistic. It should be fairly obvious that if you acquire vast quantities of property on a shoestring budget, without regard to whether they will pay for themselves, because you do not plan to keep them or because you are expecting money from some other source to help cover the operating expenses, and you continue this type of operation for an extended period, you are going to run into trouble eventually.

So, may I caution you, that while leverage and pyramiding are the tools for getting ahead in real estate, I do not advocate reckless pursuit of riches. You should be able to reach any half-way reasonable goal in less than ten years, while employing sound real estate investment practices. Just keep two feet on the ground at all times and occasionally sit down and analyze what you are accomplishing, and what you are contemplating, and analyze the effects of the move before you make any major investment decision. By keeping in close touch with your accomplishments, you will be able to keep in touch with reality.

LOOKING FOR LONG-TERM INVESTMENTS

You will, no doubt, want to acquire some properties to be held for the long term. When considering the purchase of a property you plan to hold for an extended period, some of your values will need checking. For example, you will be more concerned about the maintenance aspects of the property. Will it hold up without constant repairs and attention? Is the construction such that the cost of painting to keep it in good repair, inside and out, will not be excessive? For example, the cost of painting alone can easily vary 100 percent or more for the same size buildings when comparing a Victorian with a Contemporary design. The costs of painting or maintenance to an owner who wants the pride of ownership, and especially if he plans to live in the building, do not usually deter ownership. But for an investor who wants inexpensive maintenance and as few problems as possible, maintenance costs can be quite important. There are times however, when exceptional income potential may justify the additional trouble and expense of owning a building which would otherwise be undesirable as an investment.

All things are relative, so the key to successful carrying forward from this point is more in the analysis of the investments and relating all aspects—income, costs, and other pros and cons—of each investment, or potential investment, to that of the alternatives.

GENERAL WORDS OF CAUTION

As you progress with your investments you should be able to pick up other essential knowledge through first-hand experience. It goes without saying that you will need, at all times, to exercise due caution toward everyone and everything when making investment decisions. Not to say that you should distrust everyone, but the success of your ventures will depend a great deal on how perceptive you are. I cannot stress too strongly the importance of being alert and keeping in mind that the party on the other end of the transaction may be doing some maneuvering, or that his intentions may be less than honorable. And one of the most basic principles which should be applied to any occasion, of course, is that you should never underestimate your competitors.

Throughout this book, when I have made reference to getting a property from an owner at less than fair market value, it may sometimes sound a little as though you would be taking advantage of someone. But, I do not see it that way at all. After all, we are operating in a competitive economy based on supply and demand. Any commodity is worth what someone is willing to pay for it, and the public's opinion of the value of any particular product may vary considerably. Every purchaser is entitled to make his purchase at the lowest price available to him, providing he is not taking undue advantage of a privileged situation where he owes some special responsibility to the seller. On the same principle, the seller is entitled to get the best possible price for his product. So, in our society, the person who gets the good buy, or the good sell, usually does so through employing a keener awareness of the market conditions, or by more shrewdly negotiating the transaction. Either way, it's fair enough to keep my conscience clear. I do not feel that I have ever taken unfair advantage of anyone and I am not advocating that anyone else do so. Let your conscience be your guide.

# 18

Preparing for Retirement

Real estate investment is such an invigorating experience that it can get in the blood. Once involved, some people just can't stop themselves from continuing to delve into the mysteries and rewards of the real estate market.

But if you want, somewhere along the way, to start planning for the day when you can take it easy and enjoy the fruits of your labor, here are a few helpful hints.

The extent of your desire to disassociate yourself from further real estate activities will, of course, govern to some extent how you will want to go about arranging your retirement. Many people will consider themselves retired while they continue to manage their investments. Indeed some of you will want to continue to handle the management of your properties even after you consider yourselves more or less retired—in which case the transition from real estate investor-tycoon to semi-retired owner-manager is fairly simple.

But unless you want to spend a great deal of time fooling around with your properties, it will be necessary that they be concentrated in fairly large buildings, rather than numerous small ones. Ideally, consolidation of the properties would be accomplished gradually during the latter years of your investment career.

SELL ON THE INSTALLMENT PLAN

A good way to dispose of all management responsibilities and still have a steady income is to sell the properties on the installment plan. By accepting a maximum of 30 percent of the sales price in the first year, with a minimum of two payments extending over at least two tax years, you need only pay the capital gains tax on the portion of gain in the year you receive the payments, on a pay-as-you-receive basis. This method of selling has the advantage of postponing a good portion of your capital gains tax. Another advantage is that you are able to receive interest income on the whole balance owing. That balance would be a larger sum than you would realize from a straight sale, since funds which would have otherwise been paid out in capital gains taxes would be at work earning interest for you, and at a very good rate.

HIRE A MANAGEMENT FIRM

If you want to retain your holdings, but want to forget about most of the responsibilities of a property owner, you need only find a competent and conscientious real estate management firm to handle your investments. Many of these firms will handle everything related to the properties, including collection and deposit of all rents; overseeing all maintenance and repairs; and paying all bills, mortgages, taxes, and insurance.

In short, most property management firms will do all the work for you and will send you a quarterly accounting of the income and expenses, along with a check in the amount of the surplus funds. All this is done for a fee of approximately five percent of the gross income, though this charge is open to negotiation with many firms, depending on the type of property you own and the amount of work its management would entail. You cannot, however, expect a professional property management firm to give the close personal attention to the functions of your property that you may have given. You should be prepared for the possibility of slightly higher expenses and possibly a higher vacancy factor.

Selecting the right professional management outfit is very important since, as in all professions, there are good and bad ones. Some are not conscientious, while others are inept and unable to do a good job no matter how hard they try. Experience is an invaluable asset in effective property management. It would be a good idea to ask for references and to check the competency of a management firm in any other way you can fashion. A little research before making your decision can save you a lot of time, trouble, and money. For the first try, never sign a property management agreement for more than one year, and preferably for not more than six months. Then, in case they do not live up to your expectations, you can switch to another firm. After you are satisfied that the property management is in good hands and that your investments can get along without your direct involvement, it will be time to head for the hills, beaches, deserts, or whatever your thing happens to be, and enjoy all the adventures that you have brought within your grasp by attaining financial independence. Happy hunting!

Real Estate Terms

Adjusted gross income—The total income, less allowance for vacancy.

Agreement of sale—A written agreement whereby the purchaser agrees to buy and the seller agrees to sell certain real estate according to the terms and conditions stated therein, without transfer of title to the property until all terms and conditions of the agreement have been met.

Amenities—Any qualities that make the property desirable, such as excellent scenery or desirable social environment.

Amortization—The act or process of paying off a debt, usually by equal payments at regular intervals over a specific period of time.

Appraisal—An estimate of value.

Appreciation—Increase in value due to inflation or economic causes.

Assessed value—The value placed on property by government assessors for the purpose of levying taxes.

Balloon payment—The lump sum due upon termination of a note which has not been fully amortized.

Binder—The deposit advanced for the purpose of purchasing real estate.

Broker—A person who acts as an agent or the representative of others in real estate transactions.

Building code—Local rules regulating the construction of buildings and the standards by which all buildings are judged to be acceptable.

Capitalization—The process of converting net income into an estimated value of the property.

Closing costs—Any costs related to the purchase of real estate which must be paid before close of escrow and transfer of the property.

Cloud on the title—Any defect in the title which would need to be removed before clear title could be delivered.

Condominium—An apartment building in which the apartments are owned individually, with each owner having an individual deed.

Contract of sale—See agreement of sale.

Coop (co-operative)—An apartment building that is collectively owned and operated under one deed.

Deed—A written instrument which, when executed and delivered, conveys an estate in real estate.

Deed of trust—See trust deed.

Depreciation—A general term covering loss of value from any cause. As relating to income tax, depreciation is a yearly allowance for wear, tear, and obsolescence which will permit the taxpayer to recover his original cost over the useful life of the asset.

Duplex—A two-family house, with each dwelling unit side by side.

Easement—The right to use the land belonging to someone else. The right is a part of real estate ownership and is an encumbrance against the property over which the easement exists.

Economic life—The period of years over which a property may be profitably utilized.

Encumbrance—Anything which affects the title to property,

such as mortgages, taxes, easements, or judgments.

Equity—The interest in, or value of, real estate over and above the liens against it.

Escrow—The deposit of instruments and funds with instructions to a third neutral party to carry out the provisions of an agreement or contract. An escrow is said to be closed when everything is deposited and the transaction is consummated—usually involving transfer of title to the subject property.

Exclusive listing—A written agreement between owner and agent giving the agent the right to collect a commission if the property is sold by anyone during the term of the agreement.

F.H.A.—Federal Housing Administration. A federal government agency that insures lending institutions against loss on real estate loans, thereby providing low down payment loans. The loans constitute a higher percentage of the total value of the property than are normally available under conventional financing sources.

Fiduciary—A relationship of trust and confidence, as between principal and broker; broker as fiduciary owes a certain loyalty which cannot be breached under rules of agency.

Fixtures—Personal property which has become real estate because it is attached to real property and cannot be independently moved without agreement. Variable under state laws.

Flats—A two,- three,- or sometimes four-unit dwelling with each unit covering the whole floor either below or above the other units.

Foreclosure—Procedure whereby property pledged as security for a debt is taken from the owner in the event of default in payment or terms.

REAL ESTATE TERMS

Fringe—Along the edge.

Gross income—Total income from property before any expenses are deducted.

Highest and best use—The most profitable use to which land can be put. In appraising real estate, every parcel is entitled to be valued at its potential highest and best use.

Hold back loan—A real estate loan, a portion of which is held by the lender until certain conditions have been met, usually the performance of certain work on the property put up as security for the loan.

Impound account—A fund collected from the mortgagor to meet his tax and insurance payments when due. Required by many lenders to assure these payments.

Income property—Property held for investment, the value of which is primarily determined by the net income the property will produce.

Joint tenancy—Joint ownership by two or more persons with the right of survivorship. All joint tenants own equal interest and have equal rights in the property. Probate is avoided when property is held in joint tenancy and there is a surviving owner.

Junior mortgages (or loans)—A secondary lien which is placed on the property after a previous lien has been recorded.

Lease—A contract between owner (the lessor) and tenant (the lessee), setting forth conditions upon which the tenant may occupy and use the property.

Leverage—A term used to describe an effective use of money in acquiring property; It involves investing the least possible amount of capital in order to receive the highest possible percentage of return. It is generally accomplished by mortgaging the greatest amount that is practical; so long as mortgage payments and operating expenses are not too high, the greatest yield on capital invested can be obtained.

Lien—A specific encumbrance which makes property security for the payment of a debt or discharge of an obligation. All liens are encumbrances, but all encumbrances are not necessarily liens.

Listing—An agreement between owner and agent authorizing the agent to perform services for the owner, such as to sell or lease real estate.

Locked-in—A term used to indicate that an owner of real estate is unable to sell the property due to the inflexible nature of the existing loans, either by mortgage restrictions or by being over-financed with loans that cannot be transferred to a new owner.

Market value—The price at which a seller is willing to sell and a buyer is willing to buy, within a reasonable period of time, and with neither being under abnormal pressure to buy or sell.

Misplaced improvement—An improvement, on land, which does not conform to best utilization of the site, usually applied to a type or style of building that does not fit in with the general character of the neighborhood.

Mortgage—An instrument by which conditional transfer of title to property is effected as security for the payment of a debt or obligation.

Multiple listing—A cooperative listing, usually an exclusive right to sell, taken by a member of an organization composed of real estate brokers, with the provision that all members will have the opportunity to find an interested client.

Net income—The balance remaining after deducting from the gross income all operating expenses, maintenance, taxes, and losses pertaining to operating properties—excepting interest or other financial charges on borrowed funds.

Net listing—A listing which provides that the agent may retain as compensation for his services all sums received over and above a net price specified by the owner.

Note—A signed written instrument acknowledging a debt and promising payment. In connection with real estate, usually secured by a mortgage deed on the property.

Obsolescence—Loss in value due to reduced desirability and usefulness of a structure because its design and construction becomes out-dated and not in keeping with modern needs.

Offer—A pledge, usually in writing, to purchase certain real estate at a specified price.

Open listing—An authorization to sell a property given by the owner to a real estate agent, with the owner reserving the right to sell the property himself without obligation to the agent—sometimes qualified with the provision that the owner would be responsible for a commission to the agent in the event the property should be sold within a specified period of time to a party to whom the agent introduced the property. An open listing may be given to any number of agents without liability to compensate any except the one who secures a buyer.

Option—The right, upon payment of some form of consideration, to purchase property at a stated price within a specified time.

Party wall—A building with a common wall erected on the line between two or more adjoining properties, under one roof, which are under different ownership.

Points—The lender's charge for granting a real estate loan. A form of interest charge which can be deducted on income tax returns as interest.

Prepayment penalty—The lender's charge for accepting payment of an obligation in advance of the due date.

Principal—The employer of an agent, such as a buyer or seller, in a real estate transaction.

Probate—Property under the jurisdiction of the court (for a period of approximately six months). The sale of probate property must be for at least 90 percent of the appraised value. If property is held in joint tenancy, with one or more surviving owners, probate is avoided.

Prorate—To divide, distribute, or assess proportionately.

Purchase money mortgage—A mortgage given by the buyer in favor of the seller, which represents part of the purchase price.

Pyramiding—The process of acquiring real estate rapidly from the proceeds of sale or refinancing of other property.

Real estate—The land and everything erected on it or made a part of it or attached to it by nature or man.

Realtor—A real estate broker who is an active member of a local board having membership in the National Association of Real Estate Boards, which is dedicated to the advancement of the interests of real estate brokers and the protection of the public from unprincipled agents or brokers.

Reconveyance—To convey title back to the owner. As used herein, refers to the removal of liens on real estate.

Specific performance—A remedy by court action to require the defendant to fulfill the terms of an agreement.

Subdivision—Improved or unimproved land, divided or proposed to be divided for the purpose of sale or lease or financing, into five or more lots or parcels.

Tax base—The figure used as the property value for purposes of calculating depreciation. The tax base would be the cost, less depreciation already taken.

Tenancy in common—Ownership by two or more persons who hold undivided interest, without right of survivorship. Interests need not be equal.

Title—An instrument evidencing ownership of real estate.

Trust deed—Deed given by borrower to a trustee to be held pending fulfillment of an obligation, which is usually a loan, to the beneficiary.

INDEX

INDEX

A

Abatement Appeals Board as source of buys, 69-70
Absentee owners of properties, determining, 28-29
Ads, real estate, as source of good buys, 66
Advertising expensive for property owner, 40
Age to start investing, 18-19
Agent, selecting, 34-42
 listing property with, 37-39
 selling your own property, 39-42
Agents, avoid trusting judgments of, 27
Agreement of sale, 159-161
All-cash sale, avoid emphasis on as seller, 145-146
Anticipated income after rehabilitation, determining, 54-56
Anxiety in negotiating, avoiding, 131
Apartment buildings, conversion of into condominiums, 81
Appearances, importance of in selling property, 90-91
Appraisal fee as part of closing costs, 175
Attorneys as source of good buys, 66-67
Austerity program, initiating to build up cash reserve, 149-150
Availablity of property for sale, 141

B

Balloon payments, 120-121
Banks, foreclosures by as source of good buys, 67
Banks as source of financing, 119
Blight in area, determining cause of, 28-29
Board of Permit Appeals as source of good buys, 69-70
Borrowing money, 117-118
 purchase money mortgage, 117
Broker, selecting, 34
 (see also "Agent, selecting")
Broker's commission, borrowing for down payment, 167-168
Broker's willingness to cut commission, 147-148
Brokers, seeking area with heavy concentration of, 29-30
Brokers as source of good buys, 66
Buyers, prospective, appraising income property from viewpoint of, 52-56

C

Capital gains, 112-113
Cash. little, getting started with, 149-165
 agreement of sale, 159-161
 austerity program, initiating, 149-150
 caution, 164-165
 credit, good, importance of, 150-151
 job security, importance of, 151
 down payments, 163
 easily salable properties, sticking with, 161-162
 interest rates, shopping around for best, 163-164
 lease-option, using, 154-156
 option to purchase, cost of securing, 156-159

INDEX

Cash (*cont.*)
  reinvesting earnings, 164-165
  source of substitutes, 152-154
Cash sale, complete, avoid emphasis on as seller, 145-146
Change of market, opportunities in, 70
Closing costs, 171-175
Cluster concept, 77-79
  financing, 78-79
  fourplex, 78
Commercial property, avoiding, 63-64
Commission, broker's, borrowing for down payment, 167
  broker's willingness to cut, 147-148
Competitors, avoid underestimating 192
Complaints, tenant, 98
Concentration in one area, importance of, 26-32
Conditional sales contract for conversion to condominium, 85
Conditions for quick real estate success, 15-19
  age to start investing, 18-19
  luck, importance of, 17
  speculation, role of, 16
  time to buy, 17-18
Condominiums, profit advantages of, 75-89
  buys, good, 79-81
    apartment buildings, converting, 81
    older, used units in, 80-81
  cluster concept, 77-79
    financing, 78-79
    fourplex, 78
  conversion pointers, 84-88
    conditional sales contract, 85
    costs, careful estimation of, 88
    demand, assessing, 85-86
    planning staff, consulting local, 87
    release clause in mortgage agreement, 86
    zoning, checking, 87-88
  counsel, qualified, seeking advice of, 89
  no quick profit, 79
  over-expansion, dangers of, 76-77
  rentals, good, as good condominiums, 83
  setting, importance of, 83-84
  small investment recommended, 88-89
  who buys, 81-84
Conservatism preferable in decorating, 127-128
Consolidation of properties for later years, 193-194
Contractors, building, wariness of, 125-126
Conversion pointers for condominiums, 84-88
  (see also "Condominiums. .")
Co-operative and condominium compared, 75
Costs, need for careful estimation of in conversion to condominium, 88
Costs, unnecessary, avoiding in selling property, 91
Counteroffer of seller, limiting time of, 144
Credit, good, importance of, 150-151
  job security, importance of, 151

D

Decorating property, 122-128
  (see also "Remodeling")
Decorator, heeding advice of, 92
Demand for condominiums, assessing, 85-86
Deposit, making small when making offer, 131
Developments in area of investment, checking for, 73
"Double escrow," meaning of, 158-159

INDEX

Doubling money within year, 178-179
Down payment, generating cash for, 167-171
   broker's commission, borrowing, 167-168
   improvement loans, 170
   income tax money, 168-169
Down payments on property, 163

E

Escape clauses, avoiding when selling 142-144
Escrow fee, 172
Evaluation of area for investment, questions for, 27-30
Eviction of tenant, 108
Exchange of property, tax-free, 110-111, 181-184

F

FHA loans for financing, 118
Financing, 115-121
   balloon payments, 120-121
   borrowing money, 117-118
      purchase money mortgage, 117
   junior mortgages, 116-117
   sources of, prime, 118-120
      from banks, 119
      FHA and VA loans, 118
      "hold back loan," 120
      from insurance companies, 119-120
      savings and loan associations, 120
Financing, private, negotiating with seller to carry, 132-134
Financing for condominiums, 78-79
Firmness with tenants, maintaining, 106
Footage of area, using as appraisal method for single-family dwelling, 47-48
"For sale" signs in your area of investment, being alert for, 23
Foreclosures as source of good buys, 67
Fourplex condominium, 78

G

Gouging on rents, avoiding, 102-104
Government redevelopment areas, avoiding, 30-31
   checking into before investing, 73
Guest houses, avoiding investment in, 63-64

H

"Handy man," wariness of, 125-126
"Hippy type" of tenant, watching for, 100-101
Histories of prospective tenant's rentals, checking into, 100
Hoarding listings, practice of, 39
"Hold back loan," 120
Hotels, small, avoiding investment in, 63-64

I

"If things get tough" syndrome, avoiding, 64-65
Impound account as part of closing costs, 174-175
Improvement loans, using for down payment, 170
Improvements to property, making wise, 123-124
   building codes, checking, 124
   making them pay for themselves, 184-185
   quality workmanship, insisting on, 124
Income property, appraising, 51-61
   as buyer, prospective, 52-56

Income property, appraising (*cont.*)
  after rehabilitation, 54-56
  utility expenses, 53-54
  vacancy factor, 53
  realism, importance of, 60
  as seller, 56-61
  "times gross" method, 51-52
Income tax guidance, importance of, 109-114
  capital gains, 112-113
  impractical selling, 109-111
    exchange of property, tax-free 110-111
    personal residence, sale of, 111-112
  planning taxes, 113-114
Income tax money, using for down payment, 168-169
Installment plan, selling properties on, 194
Insurance as one of closing costs, 174
Insurance companies as source of financing, 119-120
Interest, avoid haggling about in negotiating, 137
Interest hog, seller's need to avoid becoming, 144-145

J

Job security, importance of in obtaining credit, 151
Joint ownership, 94-97
Junior mortgages, 116-117

L

Lease-option, using to buy property, 154-156, 160
Leases, possible, wariness of in negotiations, 134
Leasing, avoiding if planning to sell, 103-104
Legislation favoring tenant, coping with, 107
Leverage, 71-72, 115
  (see also "Financing")

Leverage, importance of to protect cash investments, 185
License, question of need for, 21-24
Listing property with agent, 37-39
Loan fee as part of closing costs, 173
Location for investments, selecting, 25-33
  one area, concentrating in, 26-32
  opportunities always available, 32-33
  prospects, best, 25-26
  questions regarding, 27-30
Long-term investments, looking for, 190-191
Low rents, disadvantages of, 102-103
Luck, importance of, 17
Luxury condominiums, importance of certain factors for, 84

M

Management firm, hiring to handle investments, 194-195
Management of property, 98-108
  (see also "Property management")
Manager, finding right, 99-108
Minimum cash investment, 166-179
  closing costs, 171-175
  doubling money, 178-179
  down payment, generating cash for, 167-171
    broker's commission, borrowing, 167-168
    improvement loans, 170
    income tax money, using, 168-169
  explanation, 166-167
  type of property to start with, 176-178
"Minor subdivisions," meaning of, 80

INDEX

Multi-unit buildings, smaller, more easily salable, 161-162
Multiple-family dwellings, appraising, 51-61
   as buyer, prospective, 52-56
      after rehabilitation, 54-56
      utility expenses, 53-54
      vacancy factor, 53
   as seller, 56-61
      realism, importance of, 60
      "times gross" method, 51-52

N

Neglect of property, determining cause of, 28-29
Negotiating, 129-148
   anxiety, avoiding, 131
   attorney, consultation with, 139
   broker's willingness to cut commission, 147-148
   deposit, small, 131
   interest, avoid haggling about, 137
   leases, possible, watching for, 134
   oral promise, avoid reliance on, 146-147
   price, know what included in, 134-135
   price and terms to offer, 129-131
   private financing, 132-134
      "or more" clause, inserting, 132
   to sell, 139-148
      all-cash sale, avoid emphasis on, 145-146
      availability of property, 141
      contingency pitfalls, avoiding, 142-144
      counteroffer, limiting time of, 144
      interest hog, avoid becoming, 144-145
      offers, phony, wariness of, 141
      price, setting your own, 140-141

      seller's reason for selling, considering, 136-139
      title insurance, 135-136
Newer areas not prime investment prospects, 26
"No growth" policies, 76
Non-exclusive listing, 38

O

Offers to buy, phony, wariness of, 141
Older areas prime areas for investments, 25-26
Older people prime buyers of condominiums, 82-83
Open listing, 38
Option to purchase, cost of securing, 156-159
"Or more" clause, inserting in mortgage contract, 132
Over-expansion of condominiums, danger of, 76-77
Over-improvement of property, avoiding, 124
Ownership of real estate, tax advantages of, 181

P

Paintings, renting, to improve appearance of house for sale, 90-91
Partner, involvement with, 93-97
   joint ownership, 94-97
   silent partner best, 93-94
Population growth, area of as best investment, 32-33
Prepayment penalties, 114, 132-133
Price, determining best, 43-61
   income property, 51-61
      as buyer, prospective, 52-56
      (see also "Income property . . . . . .")
      realism, importance of, 60
      as seller, 56-61
      "times gross" method, 51-52

Price (*cont.*)
   single-family dwelling, appraising, 47-51
Price to offer in negotiating, 129-131
Principal, meaning of, 22
Private financing, 132-134
Probate sales, 67-69
Profit advantages of condominiums, 75-89 (see also "Condominiums, profit advantages of")
Property, listing of, 37-39
Property management, 98-108
   manager, finding right, 99-108
   screening tenants, 99-101
   tenant complaints, handling, 98
Proration of interest at closing, 172-173
Prospects, best, 25-26
Protecting cash investments, 180-192
   caution, 191-192
   exchange, tax-free 181-184
   familiar areas, sticking to, 180
   improvements, justification of expenditure for, 184-185
   leverage, 185
   long-term investments, seeking, 190-191
   pyramiding, 185-190
   tax advantages of ownership of, 181
Purchase money mortgages, 117
Pyramiding, 185-190

Q

Qualities of area, evaluating before investing, 27-30

R

Real estate brokers, presence of as indication of land activity, 29-30
Reason of seller for selling, considering, 136-137
Recklessness, avoiding, 189-190
Redevelopment areas, avoiding, 30-31
Release clause in mortgage agreement for condominiums, 86
Remodeling, 122-128
   contractors, wariness of, 125-126
   decorating, 126-128
   improvements, making right, 123-124
   over-improvements, avoiding, 124
   workmanship, insisting on right, 124
Remodeling, limiting, in sale of property 91-92
Rent gouging, 102
Rent strike, how to handle threatened, 103-104
Rental agreements, 105
Rentals, good as good condominium possibilities, 83
Rents, setting, 102
Repair of property, maintaining, 106-107
Residence, personal, sale of, 111-112
Residence clubs, avoiding, 63-64
Residential property most easily sold 161-162
Resort properties, avoiding, 65-66
Retirement, preparing for, 193-195
   installment plan, selling on, 194
   management firm, hiring, 194-195
Right time to buy, 17-18

S

Salability of house, determining, 48
Sale of property, preparing for, 90-92
   appearances, importance of, 90-91
   costs, unnecessary, avoiding, 91

INDEX

Sale of Property (*con't.*)
  remodeling, limiting, 91-92
Savings and loan associations as source of financing, 119
Screening of prospective tenants, 99-101
Seller, analyzing income property from viewpoint of, 56-61
Seller carrying mortgage, 132-134
Selling, impractical, 109-111
Selling, tips for, 139-148 (see also "Negotiating")
Senior citizens, appeal of condominiums to, 82-83
75 percent to 80 percent loan, 163
Silent partner best, 93-94
Single-family dwelling, appraising, 47-51
Small investment in condominiums recommended, 88-89
Sources of good buys, 62-74
  commercial property, avoiding, 63-64
  "if things should get tough" syndrome, avoiding, 64-65
  resort properties, avoiding, 65-66
  syndications, real estate, avoiding, 65
  tips, 66-74
    attorneys, 66-67
    bad times, taking advantage of, 70
    banks and savings and loan institutions, 67
    brokers, 66
    probate sales, 67-69
    unimproved land, avoiding, 62-63
Spare time investing, 20-24
  license, need for, 21-24
Specializing as key to finding good buys, 62

Speculation, need of for success, 16-17
Square footage, using for appraisals, 47-48
Student loans, use of to raise cash for investment, 170
Syndications, real estate, avoiding, 65

T

Tax advantages of real estate ownership, 181
Tax guidance, income, 109-114 (see also "Income tax guidance ......")
Tax-free exchange of property, 110-111, 181-184
Taxes, planning, 113-114
Tenant complaints, proper handling of, 98
Terms to offer in negotiating, 129-131
Thirty-day open listing, 38
"Times gross" income, meaning of, 51
Title insurance, 135-136
Title to property, agreement of sale and, 159-161

U

Unfamiliar areas of investment, avoiding, 180
Unimproved land, avoiding, 62-63

V

VA loans, 118, 160-161
Vacancy factor, 53

W

Workmanship, insisting on quality of, 124